Securing the future

In 1999 my government first set out our strategy to help deliver a better quality of life through sustainable development. Six years on we have reviewed that strategy to take account of changes within the UK – devolution to Scotland and Wales, and to regional bodies and local government – and internationally with the World Summit on Sustainable Development in 2002.

Make the wrong choices now and future generations will live with a changed climate, depleted resources and without the green space and biodiversity that contribute both to our standard of living and our quality of life. Each of us needs to make the right choices to secure a future that is fairer, where we can all live within our environmental limits. That means sustainable development.

This is an agenda for the long-term. There is no magic wand that government or any one else can wave to make sustainable behaviour and activity the norm overnight. We will only succeed if we go with the grain of what individuals and businesses want, and channel their creativity to confront the environmental challenges we face. Development, growth, and prosperity need not and should not be in conflict with sustainability.

Over the past six years scientific opinion has moved decisively to an almost universal consensus that climate change is happening and is the result of human activity. That means we can move the debate from whether there is a problem to how to deal with it. Yes, climate change represents a potentially catastrophic threat, but it is within our control to address it – and address it we must. Climate change will not only affect the UK but all parts of the world, and it stands to most damage those areas least able to adapt to it particularly sub-Saharan Africa. However, we must also respond to this challenge at home. Our 2003 Energy White Paper set us on a clear path to a low carbon economy. Our task now is to deliver at home and find ways to get international agreement through the G8 and other forums to strengthen the global effort to tackle climate change.

Although climate change is the most serious global environmental threat, promoting new, modern, sustainable ways of living, working, producing and travelling also stand to achieve wider benefits to human health and well being. We need to maintain our duty of care towards our natural resources, for our own benefit and for the benefit of future generations.

We are increasingly aware of the need to make care for the environment an integral part of policy making from the start, rather than dealing with the consequences of neglect down the line. We need to regard the local environment as a major public service (like the NHS or education) which benefits us every day. Looked at this way, it is clear why policies to promote better quality environments also have the capacity to have long-term social and economic benefits. Often those people who are most economically and socially disadvantaged also live in degraded environments with fewer jobs, unsafe and ugly streets. Our goals are a strong economy, and decent homes in places with clean, safe and green public spaces, where people are able to lead healthy lives, and enjoy the environment around them. So our new strategy contains not only a commitment to create sustainable communities but a commitment to give a new focus to tackling environmental inequalities as well.

The response to the consultation for this strategy made clear that what was needed in this strategy was a move into action. So the strategy includes clear actions to promote sustainability by involving people, leading by example and by demonstrating our commitment to deliver:

▶ Our new Community Action 2020 programme will give people the opportunity in every community in the country to make a difference locally – or globally. We have seen what some communities have done with Local Agenda 21 – I want to see that energy, throughout the country, coming up with local solutions and actions – on transport, on waste, on energy and on creating places where people want to live

▶ Government will lead by example. The UK Government buys £13 billion worth of goods and services each year. For the wider public sector this figure is £125 billion. We want to ensure that we spend your money sustainably, starting with a commitment to buy cleaner cars and by our new offsetting scheme to reduce the carbon impacts of unavoidable air travel. In this document we show how every government department will contribute to this strategy. I want every government department to produce its own action plan by the end of the year so we can ensure delivery

▶ To show we are serious about delivery, we will stop reporting our own progress and hand that task over to a strengthened Sustainable Development Commission, which will act as the independent "watchdog" of government progress.

This is a truly challenging agenda. It will involve working across departmental boundaries and through all levels of government – from the neighbourhood to the United Nations. It involves channelling the power of business by stimulating the market to innovate and to produce more cost effective and sustainable options for all purchasers. It needs the commitment of voluntary groups, and it involves influencing the individual everyday choices we all make.

Most of all, it means focussing on long-term solutions, not short-term fixes. Targeting prevention now, rather than putting right later. Ensuring we get the full environmental, social and economic dividend from every pound we spend.

We have spent a long time getting to grips with the concept of sustainability. I want to declare a moratorium on further words. I want this new strategy to be a catalyst for action to secure our future.

Tony Blair

The UK G
Developm

Presented to Parliament by the Secretary of State
for Environment, Food and Rural Affairs
by Command of Her Majesty
March 2005

Cm 6467

£26

Index of chapters

Executive Summary

Our Strategy for sustainable development aims to enable all people throughout the world to satisfy their basic needs and enjoy a better quality of life without compromising the quality of life of future generations.

Chapter 1:

A new strategy

The Government has a new purpose and principles for sustainable development and new shared priorities agreed across the UK, including the Devolved Administrations. The strategy contains:

> ❯ a new integrated vision building on the 1999 strategy – with stronger international and societal dimensions

> ❯ five principles – with a more explicit focus on environmental limits

> ❯ four agreed priorities – sustainable consumption and production, climate change, natural resource protection and sustainable communities, and

> ❯ a new indicator set, which is more outcome focused, with commitments to look at new indicators such as on wellbeing.

Chapter 2:

Helping people make better choices

We all – governments, businesses, public sector, voluntary and community organisations, communities and families – need to make different choices if we are to achieve the vision of sustainable development.

The Government proposes a new approach to influencing behaviours based on recent research on what determines current patterns. The Government will focus on measures to enable and encourage behaviour change, measures to engage people, and ways in which the Government can lead by example. Where these are not sufficient to change entrenched habits, we will also look for ways to catalyse changes.

Key commitments include:

> ❯ a new programme of community engagement – Community Action 2020 – Together We Can – to act as a catalyst for community action helping people to get involved by providing skills training, improved access to funding and mentors

> ❯ a deliberative forum to look at what it would take to help people live more sustainable lifestyles

> ❯ piloting open and innovative ways to allow stakeholders to influence decisions about the kind of projects which would deliver the goals of this strategy

> ❯ new commitments to support education and training in sustainable development, and

> ❯ evaluations of key environmental taxes to help build a more comprehensive picture of the effectiveness of such taxes and inform further reviews, including that of the Climate Change Programme.

Chapter 3:

"One planet economy": sustainable consumption and production

Increasing prosperity, in the UK and across the world, has allowed many people to enjoy the benefits of goods and services which were once available to just a few. We have also made progress in cleaning up some of the worst industrial pollution. Nevertheless, the environmental impacts of our consumption and production patterns remain severe, and inefficient use of resources is a drag on the UK economy and businesses. In addition, internationally we need to promote the mutual supportiveness of trade liberalisation, environmental protection and sustainable development to help developing countries.

We need a major shift to deliver new products and services with lower environmental impacts across their lifecycle, and new business models which meet this challenge while boosting competitiveness. And we need to build on people's growing awareness of social and environmental concerns, and the importance of their roles as citizens and consumers.

Our strategy for doing this involves:

➤ strengthening UK and international measures to improve the environmental performance of products and services, including improved product design

➤ a continued drive to improve resource efficiency and reduce waste and harmful emissions across business sectors, aided by the new Business Resource Efficiency and Waste (BREW) programme

➤ a new push to influence consumption patterns, including proposals for new advice for consumers

➤ new commitments on sustainable procurement in the public sector to make the UK a leader within the EU by 2009

➤ support for innovation to bring through new products, materials and services

➤ stronger partnerships with key business sectors such as the food, tourism and construction industries, and

➤ a review of our waste strategy, with increased emphasis on reducing waste at source and making use of it as a resource.

Chapter 4:

Confronting the greatest threat: climate change and energy

The UK government is committed to reducing the country's greenhouse gas emissions. In its 2003 Energy White Paper, the Government put the goal of moving to a low carbon economy at the heart of its energy strategy, and set out a long term goal of reducing carbon dioxide emissions by some 60 per cent by about 2050, with real progress to be shown by 2020.

In addition, we have a target under the Kyoto Protocol to reduce greenhouse gas emissions by 12.5 per cent below base year levels by 2008-12, and a more ambitious national goal of reducing carbon dioxide emissions by 20 per cent below 1990 levels by 2010. Our Climate Change Programme sets out policies and measures to help achieve these goals.

The UK is on track to meet its Kyoto target – a significant achievement. However, more needs to be done to achieve our national 2010 goal. Through the current review of the UK Climate Change Programme the Government is committed to evaluating the existing programme measures and aims to publish a revised programme in summer 2005.

Major international and domestic developments which are already in the pipeline include:

▶ putting climate change as a top priority for both the UK's G8 and European Union presidencies in 2005

▶ discussion at an international level on further engagement of all parties to the United Nations Framework Convention on Climate Change on future action to reduce greenhouse gas emissions, and adaptation strategies

▶ launch of the Climate Change Communications Initiative with funding of at least £12 million over the period 2005-08, to tackle public attitudes to, and understanding of, climate change, and what we can each do to help reduce our personal contribution to climate change

▶ delivering against our commitments in 'Energy Efficiency: The Government's Plan for Action'

▶ a consultation on the draft code for sustainable buildings during 2005, with national rollout planned to begin in 2006

▶ launch of the Government's pilot carbon offsetting scheme for air travel in 2005

▶ pressing for the inclusion of intra-EU air services in the EU emissions trading scheme from 2008 or as soon as possible thereafter; this will be a priority for the UK Presidency of the EU in 2005, and

▶ publication of a climate change adaptation policy framework during 2005.

Chapter 5:

A future without regrets: protecting our natural resources and enhancing the environment

Natural resources are vital to our existence and to the development of communities throughout the world.

The issues we face are the need for better understanding of environmental limits, the need for environmental enhancement where the environment is most degraded, the need to ensure a decent environment for everyone, and the need for a more integrated policy framework to deliver this.

Key commitments in the strategy include:

> producing an integrated policy approach for protecting and enhancing natural resources with stakeholders in 2005

> researching environmental limits and environmental inequalities

> taking account of natural systems as a whole, through the use of an ecosystems approach

> bringing together all the UK Government's policy frameworks, targets and strategies for natural resources

> modernising the delivery framework through the creation of new agencies to manage the marine and terrestrial environments

> launching Environmental Stewardship to incentivise farmers to deliver environmental benefits

> addressing problems of degraded resources and environmental inequalities by enhancing the role of the Environment Agency, the creation of the Integrated Agency, and by strategic partnership work nationally and locally between Defra and the Department of Health and their agencies

> working with international partners to reduce the rate of biodiversity loss worldwide, and

> encouraging partner countries globally to integrate principles of sustainable development into poverty reduction and development processes, assisting developing countries in negotiation and implementation of Multilateral Environmental Agreements, and supporting multilateral institutions such as the UN Environment Programme.

Chapter 6:

From local to global: creating sustainable communities and a fairer world

The Government will promote joined-up solutions to locally identified problems, working in partnership to tackle economic, social and environmental issues.

At the local level, we are announcing a package of measures to realise the vision of sustainable communities across England, in both urban and rural areas, which will catalyse the delivery of sustainable development.

At the national level, the strategy sets out the framework for changing people's lives through improvements in public services and providing opportunity for all.

At the global level, we look at how we will apply the principles of good governance, democracy and partnership and how to work effectively to meet locally identified priorities so that this country helps meet Millennium Development Goals.

Key commitments include:

> joining up effectively at the local level around the vision of sustainable communities with Sustainable Community Strategies and Local Area Agreements, linked to planning through Local Development Frameworks

> placing sustainable development at the heart of the land use planning system and at the core of new planning guidance

> enabling people to participate fully by providing new neighbourhood structures and funding to allow people to have a say in the way their neighbourhoods are run

> new powers for local authorities under the Clean Neighbourhoods and Environment Bill

> meeting the new national target to improve the local environment, focused on the most deprived neighbourhoods

> providing better information to people on their local environment

> creating opportunities locally for people to improve their local environment, health, education, job prospects, and housing

> helping to improve international environmental governance including through continued support for the Partnership for Principle 10, and

> working with other donors to increase global levels of official development assistance, including through the International Finance Facility.

Chapter 7:

Ensuring it happens

We want to ensure that this strategy is converted into action. We are proposing additional measures, which we believe will prove powerful catalysts for improved delivery:

> strengthening the Sustainable Development Commission and asking it to report on the Government's progress on sustainable development

> mainstreaming sustainable development in the Civil Service through the Professional Skills In Government programme and embedding sustainable development into the curriculum of the National School of Government, to be launched in the first half of 2005

> establishing an Academy for Sustainable Communities and launching a new 'How To' programme to promote the take up and use of new and existing powers to transform the local environment

> working with the Audit Commission to strengthen the Comprehensive Performance Assessment of local authorities to take more account of sustainable development and the local environment

➤ all central Government departments and their executive agencies will produce focused sustainable development action plans based on this strategy by December 2005

➤ reviewing the effectiveness of arrangements to deliver sustainable development at the regional level

➤ a new Sustainable Development Programme as part of the UK's Global Opportunities Fund, complemented by additional Defra funding to help deliver commitments from the World Summit on Sustainable Development, and

➤ monitoring more effectively delivery of the UK's international sustainable development priorities.

Chapter 1
A New Strategy

1. Why sustainable development?

The past 20 years have seen a growing realisation that the current model of development is unsustainable.

On the one hand we see the increasing burden our way of life places on the planet on which we depend:

> the consequences of already unavoidable climate change

> increasing stress on resources and environmental systems – water, land and air – from the way we produce, consume and waste resources, and

> increasing loss of biodiversity from the rainforest to the stocks of fish around our coast.

"We know the problems. A child in Africa dies every three seconds from famine, disease or conflict. We know that if climate change is not stopped, all parts of the world will suffer. Some will even be destroyed, and we know the solution – sustainable development."

Rt. Hon. Tony Blair MP, Prime Minister, speech to the World Summit on Sustainable Development

On the other hand we see a world where over a billion people live on less than a dollar a day, more than 800 million are malnourished, and over two and a half billion lack access to adequate sanitation. A world disfigured by poverty and inequality is unsustainable. While increasing wealth is most often associated with depletion of environmental resources, extreme poverty can also leave people with no option but to deplete their local environment – so sustainable poverty eradication depends on the poor having access to adequate natural resources and a healthy environment.

Unless we start to make real progress toward reconciling these contradictions, we all, wherever we live, face a future that is less certain and less secure than we in the UK have enjoyed over the past fifty years. We need to make a decisive move towards more sustainable development both because it is the right thing to do, and because it is in our long-term best interests. It offers the best hope for securing the future.

Our starting point

At the Rio summit in 1992, governments around the world committed to sustainable development. The UK government was the first to produce its national strategy in 1994. In 1999, the UK government then outlined how it proposed to deliver sustainable development in 'A Better Quality of Life'. This set out a vision of simultaneously delivering economic, social and environmental outcomes as measured by a series of headline indicators.

Since 1999 progr ss has been measured every year against these indicators. Some have moved very much in the right direction: the UK has maintained strong economic performance, enjoying an unbroken period of economic growth throughout. A strong economy can bring many benefits – it supports jobs, pays for the public services on which we rely, and is key to poverty eradication. Economic stability also helps to avoid the waste of human and physical resources that comparatively sluggish economic performance inevitably brings. It is a factor in achieving a more just society, and directly contributes to personal wellbeing.

But we cannot be complacent about the positive trends. Income is not the only component of people's wellbeing. Good health, a safe environment and strong communities are also very important. In some areas, the indicators have moved in the wrong direction – the amount of waste we generate continues to rise, although the trend is slowing. Reducing the impacts of road traffic remains a significant challenge, despite some weakening in the relationship between road traffic and economic growth. Farmland and woodland bird populations, proxies for the wider state of our wildlife, show signs of stabilising, but recovery is needed.

Our performance to date can be summed up by the comments of the Sustainable Development Commission in their review of the progress since 1999, published in April 2004: 'Shows Promise, But Must Try Harder'. The Commission applauded our progress in many areas but also identified twenty key areas in which we need to take more decisive action for the new strategy and in the years to follow.

This new strategy responds to that challenge. It takes account of developments here since 1999: the changed structure of government in the UK with devolution to Scotland, Wales and Northern Ireland; greater emphasis on delivery at regional level and the new relationship between government and local authorities. It takes account of new policies announced since 1999, in particular the 2003 Energy White Paper that sets a long-term goal of achieving a low carbon economy. It also takes account of the renewed international push for sustainable development from the World Summit on Sustainable Development in Johannesburg in 2002, and the Millennium Development Goals set out in 2000, due for review later this year (2005).

It has been developed within a common framework for the UK, agreed between the UK government and the Devolved Administrations for Scotland, Wales and Northern Ireland. Within this framework they will set out their strategies for delivering sustainable development in the areas for which they are responsible. This UK strategy sets out what the UK government proposes to do in England and in the areas for which it retains responsibility in the UK, including international relations.

We have benefited from the many responses received from the consultation 'Taking it on'[1]. These took many forms and included 900 written and electronic responses to the document, more than twenty themed workshops organised for us by organisations with an interest in sustainable development from across the UK, nine regional dialogue events in England, and local community consultations assisted by trained facilitators. We are indebted to everyone who took time to contribute their thoughts and ideas, which they will see reflected in this document.

This strategy has been developed across government – both central government departments and with regional and local partners. We have also benefited greatly from the advice and help of the Sustainable Development Commission throughout this process.

The key message emerging from the consultation was that this strategy needed to make a real change from talking about sustainable development to delivering it on the ground. This new strategy shows how we propose to do that to secure the future – for all of us.

2. The strategic framework

In the consultation on the new UK Sustainable Development Strategy we committed ourselves to produce a UK strategic framework for sustainable development covering the period up to 2020. This has been agreed by the UK Government and the Devolved Administrations in Scotland, Wales and Northern Ireland, to provide a consistent approach and focus across the UK.

This framework, launched in conjunction with the UK Government Strategy, includes:

➤ a shared understanding of sustainable development

➤ a vision of what we are trying to achieve and the guiding principles we all need to follow to achieve it

➤ our sustainable development priorities for UK action at home and internationally, and

➤ indicators to monitor the key issues on a UK basis.

Delivering the Framework

The strategic framework will be supported by separate strategies for each administration. These will build on existing work and translate the framework's aims into action, based on their different responsibilities, needs and views. The strategies of the UK and Devolved Administrations will include further priorities, and be supported by further measures and indicators.

[1] A Defra summary report of the consultation is available on the Government's sustainable development website: www.sustainable-development.gov.uk/taking-it-on/finalsummary.htm

UK Strategic Framework			
UK Government Strategy*	Welsh Assembly Action Plan	Scottish Executive Strategy	Northern Ireland Strategy

*Covers England and all non-devolved issues, including international relations

3. A common purpose

"Living on the earth's income rather than eroding its capital"

quotation from the 'Taking it on' consultation response from e3 Consulting

To set the United Kingdom on a more sustainable track, we must know what we are aiming for. The 1999 strategy set out clearly that sustainable development means "a better quality of life for everyone, now and for generations to come", and used the widely used international definition "development which meets the needs of the present without compromising the ability of future generations to meet their own needs."[2]

The four central aims of the 1999 strategy were:

➤ social progress which recognises the needs of everyone

➤ effective protection of the environment

➤ prudent use of natural resources, and

➤ maintenance of high and stable levels of economic growth and employment.

These aims effectively captured the simple priority areas at the heart of sustainable development. However, although the 1999 strategy stressed that these objectives had to be pursued at the same time, in practice, different agencies focused on those one or two most relevant to them. So a new purpose is needed to show how government will integrate these aims and evolve sustainable development policy – to develop the earlier Strategy, not depart from it. It needs to paint a picture of what things should look like if we achieve sustainable development, while maintaining continuity with the aims of the 1999 Strategy.

The following 'purpose', which has been agreed by the UK Government and the Devolved Administrations, has now been adopted as the new framework goal for sustainable development:

[2] From 'Our Common Future (The Brundtland Report)' – Report of the 1987 World Commission on Environment and Development.

The goal of sustainable development is to enable all people throughout the world to satisfy their basic needs and enjoy a better quality of life, without compromising the quality of life of future generations.

For the UK Government and the Devolved Administrations, that goal will be pursued in an integrated way through a sustainable, innovative and productive economy that delivers high levels of employment; and a just society that promotes social inclusion, sustainable communities and personal wellbeing. This will be done in ways that protect and enhance the physical and natural environment, and use resources and energy as efficiently as possible.

Government must promote a clear understanding of, and commitment to, sustainable development so that all people can contribute to the overall goal through their individual decisions.

Similar objectives will inform all our international endeavours, with the UK actively promoting multilateral and sustainable solutions to today's most pressing environmental, economic and social problems. There is a clear obligation on more prosperous nations both to put their own house in order, and to support other countries in the transition towards a more equitable and sustainable world.

4. Guiding principles

The following is the set of shared UK principles that we will use to achieve our sustainable development purpose. These have been agreed by the UK Government, Scottish Executive, Welsh Assembly Government and the Northern Ireland Administration. They bring together and build on the various previously existing UK principles to set out an overarching approach, which the four separate strategies can share.

Living Within Environmental Limits

Respecting the limits of the planet's environment, resources and biodiversity – to improve our environment and ensure that the natural resources needed for life are unimpaired and remain so for future generations.

Ensuring a Strong, Healthy and Just Society

Meeting the diverse needs of all people in existing and future communities, promoting personal wellbeing, social cohesion and inclusion, and creating equal opportunity for all.

Achieving a Sustainable Economy

Building a strong, stable and sustainable economy which provides prosperity and opportunities for all, and in which environmental and social costs fall on those who impose them (polluter pays), and efficient resource use is incentivised.

Promoting Good Governance

Actively promoting effective, participative systems of governance in all levels of society – engaging people's creativity, energy, and diversity.

Using Sound Science Responsibly

Ensuring policy is developed and implemented on the basis of strong scientific evidence, whilst taking into account scientific uncertainty (through the precautionary principle) as well as public attitudes and values.

"*[The revised sustainable development strategy] should provide a framework of principles which are applied to every area of policy in every department – a lens through which all proposals are viewed.*"

quotation from the 'Taking it on' consultation response from WWF-UK

These principles will form the basis for policy in the UK. For a policy to be sustainable, it must respect all five of these principles, though we recognise that some policies, while underpinned by all five, will place more emphasis on certain principles than others. Any trade-offs should be made in an explicit and transparent way. We want to achieve our goals of living within environmental limits and a just society, and we will do it by means of a sustainable economy, good governance, and sound science.

5. Shared priorities for UK action

As a result of the consultation the priority areas for immediate action, shared across the UK are:

Sustainable Consumption and Production – Sustainable consumption and production is about achieving more with less. This means not only looking at how goods and services are produced, but also the impacts of products and materials across their whole lifecycle and building on people's awareness of social and environmental concerns. This includes reducing the inefficient use of resources which are a drag on the economy, so helping boost business competitiveness and to break the link between economic growth and environmental degradation.

Climate Change and Energy – The effects of a changing climate can already be seen. Temperatures and sea levels are rising, ice and snow cover are declining, and the consequences could be catastrophic for the natural world and society. Scientific evidence points to the release of greenhouse gases, such as carbon dioxide and methane, into the atmosphere by human activity as the primary cause of climatic change. We will seek to secure a profound change in the way we generate and use energy, and in other activities that release these gases. At the same time we must prepare for the climate change that cannot now be avoided. We must set a good example and will encourage others to follow it.

Natural Resource Protection and Environmental Enhancement – Natural resources are vital to our existence and that of communities throughout the world. We need a better understanding of environmental limits, environmental enhancement and recovery where the environment is most degraded to ensure a decent environment for everyone, and a more integrated policy framework.

Sustainable Communities – Our aim is to create sustainable communities that embody the principles of sustainable development at the local level. This will involve working to give communities more power and say in the decisions that affect them; and working in partnership at the right level to get things done. The UK uses the same principles of engagement, partnership, and programmes of aid in order to tackle poverty and environmental degradation and to ensure good governance in overseas communities.

These priorities for action within the UK will also help to shape the way the UK works internationally, in ensuring that our objectives and activities are aligned with international goals.

6. Priorities for international action

Our strategic objective for international sustainable development is to support multilateral and national institutions that can ensure effective integration of social, environmental and economic objectives to deliver sustainable development, especially for the poorest members of society.

"Sustainable development is about much more than just bringing the environment into development. If things are going to change, what we need is not abstract notions, nor doom and gloom, but practical, effective and above all fair principles for the sound management of the planet. Because development that's sustainable has to work for the poor as well as for the planet".

Rt. Hon. Hilary Benn MP, Secretary of State, Department for International Development

The UK's international priorities on sustainable development since the UK's 1999 Sustainable Development Strategy have principally been framed by the Millennium Development Goals (MDGs), the Doha Development Agenda of the World Trade Organisation, the Monterrey Consensus on Financing for Development and the Plan of Implementation of the 2002 World Summit on Sustainable Development (WSSD). These built on pre-existing commitments including those from the Rio Earth Summit of 1992 and other international processes including Multilateral Environmental Agreements.

The WSSD outcomes complement the MDGs, reinforce Doha and Monterrey agreements and set challenging global goals and targets on accessing water, sanitation and modern energy services; increasing energy efficiency and use of renewable energy; sustainable fisheries and forests; reducing biodiversity loss on land and in our oceans; chemicals management; and decoupling environmental degradation from economic growth – that is, achieving sustainable patterns of consumption and production.

International commitments must be followed up and implemented as a matter of urgency. This must be done through addressing the international impacts of our domestic policies and by working with developed and developing countries, and international institutions, to spread good practice and maintain political pressure for change.

The diagram opposite outlines the international priorities, drawing a distinction between goals, targets and the means of achieving them. UK policies and actions to help achieve these international objectives are set out in later chapters.

Priorities for Action on International Sustainable Development this Millennium

Key International Summits

The Millennium Assembly of the UN – New York 2000

UK pledged with 190 UN Member States to implement the Millennium Declaration, supported by eight Millennium Development Goals (MDGs) on poverty, illiteracy, hunger, lack of education, gender inequality, child and maternal mortality, disease and environmental sustainability.

The Fourth WTO Ministerial Conference Doha 2001

The international community agreed to promote trade liberalisation, focusing on the needs of developing countries and progressing the goal of sustainable development. Focus on building and maintaining an open and non-discriminatory multi-lateral trading system.

International Conference on Financing for Development – Monterrey 2002

World leaders agreed to mobilise and increase the effective use of financial resources and achieve economic conditions for poverty reduction and sustained economic growth

The World Summit on Sustainable Development (WSSD) – Johannesburg 2002

The WSSD outcomes complemented the MDGs, reinforced Doha and Monterrey agreements and set challenging global goals and targets

---

The commitments/targets are interdependent.
Many were agreed upon at one summit but were reinforced and built upon at subsequent events.

Commitments / Targets

MDG1 Eradicate extreme poverty and hunger

MDG3 Achieve universal primary education

MDG2 Promote gender equality; empower women

MDG5 Reduce child mortality

MDG4 Improve maternal health

MDG6 Combat AIDS, malaria & other diseases

MDG 7 Ensure Environmental Sustainability

MDG8 Develop a global partnership for development

Extend an open and rules based multi-lateral trading system

Improve market access for developing countries

Promote mutual supportiveness of trade liberalisation, environmental protection and sustainable development

Minimise any negative impacts of trade liberalisation for developing countries

Reduce level of trade distorting subsidies, particularly in agriculture and fisheries

Increase aid volumes and predictability of financial and technical assistance

Donor co-operation and harmonisation

Aligning international finance with country-owned development plans

Untying aid

Strengthening developing country voice in international finance decision making

Integrated water resource management plans

Minimise adverse effects of chemicals on human health and environment by 2020

Provide reliable and affordable energy services

Halve proportion of people without access to drinking water and basic sanitation by 2015

Reaffirmed target under MDG7 to achieve by 2020 a significant improvement in the lives of at least 100 million slum dwellers

Strengthen forest law enforcement and governance

Networks of marine protected areas by 2012

Reverse natural resource loss

Significantly reduce rate of biodiversity loss by 2010

Restore depleted fish stocks by 2015; urgent action on illegal fishing

Develop a 10-year framework of sustainable consumption and production programmes

More sustainable patterns of consumption and production

Urge countries to ratify the Kyoto protocol

Urgently and substantially increase global use of renewable energy; increase energy efficiency

---

Tools/Actions to deliver the above commitments are mutually supportive and cross cutting

Actively promote corporate social responsibility

Partnerships

Key Tools

Capacity Building

Help developing countries to adjust to liberalisation through trade related capacity building and technical assistance

Encourage, through liberalisation, the trade in environmental goods and services

Sharing knowledge, increasing scientific understanding and co-operating on technology

Promote the empowerment of people living in poverty and their organisations

Promote women's access to and participation in decision making at all levels

Institutional capacity building

Good Governance at all levels

MDG7 Integrate sustainable development into countries policies and programmes

Strengthen developing country ownership

Tackle corruption, improve transparency

Improve security and reduce conflict

Promote freedom of information, public participation in decision making and the rule of law

Mainstream sustainable development in UN and international finance institutions

Sustainability impact assessments

Encourage Inter-agency co-operation

Strengthen international environmental governance

National sustainable development strategies or equivalent by 2005

Finance

Sustainable debt financing

Innovative sources of financing including International Finance Facility

Well-targeted aid addressing country needs

Sustainable development at the EU level

The key objectives that the European Union's Sustainable Development Strategy (EU SDS) has set out to tackle are climate change, natural resource protection, sustainable transport, ageing population, public health and the global dimension of sustainable development. We are committed to addressing these objectives through the UK Strategy and other domestic programmes.

In Europe our aim, which will be a focus for our presidency in the second half of 2005, will be to take forward efforts to deliver sustainable development and to forge links between the economic, social and environmental agendas. The current review of the EU SDS is an important opportunity to take this agenda forward and to provide a framework for integrating sustainable development into all EU processes and policies. We want to see a strong and ambitious EU Strategy that delivers an innovative, highly competitive, resource efficient, low carbon economy that provides an excellent quality of life for all its citizens and a mutually beneficial relationship with its trading partners. This should be achieved in harmony with the protection of human health and the environment, and can be delivered by:

> a more effective integration of global commitments and actions into the core of the strategy

> measurement of progress against a core set of priority targets, most of which are already in place

> a focus on delivery of existing commitments plus reform where indicators continue to show that we are not moving in a sustainable direction

> measures to embed sustainable development at all levels of decision-making and across all policy sectors

> encouragement of more effective learning between Member States, and

> commitment to a more active involvement of stakeholders, especially in the impact assessment of new policies.

The UK will deploy its resources in order to promote sustainable development across the full range of the EU's policies.

7. Indicators for the UK Government Strategy

We are introducing a new set of high-level indicators: the **UK Framework Indicators** to give an overview of sustainable development and the priority areas in the UK.

Responses from the consultation 'Taking it on' showed that there remained strong support for an overarching set of UK 'headline' indicators, even though since devolution there have been separate indicators sets for Wales and Scotland and a set under development in Northern Ireland.

The UK Framework indicators are intended to cover key impacts and outcomes that reflect the priority areas shared across the UK.

In addition to the shared UK Framework Indicators there will be a mix of indicators, targets and performance measures in the individual strategies for the UK Government, Scotland, Wales and Northern Ireland. These will underpin the shared framework priorities while reflecting the respective priorities of each administration.

Indicators for the UK Government Strategy include all 20 of the UK Framework Indicators and a further 48 indicators related to the priority areas. Relevant indicators are listed at the end of each chapter. The full list of 68 indicators is presented in Chapter 7, along with related Public Service Agreement targets, and national strategies.

We will assess and report annually on progress against the indicators and use this assessment, together with other evidence from monitoring and evaluation, to determine whether we are succeeding in our goals or whether we need to develop different policies and act accordingly.

Criteria for the set of indicators

In selecting the new UK Framework Indicators, we have chosen measures that wherever possible:

➤ are **linked** to the purpose and priorities within the UK Framework

➤ are **agreed** as high priorities by the UK Government and Devolved Administrations

➤ have **UK coverage** (though there are some data constraints)

➤ have **trends** available

➤ highlight **challenges**, and

➤ are statistically **robust and meaningful**.

The same criteria apply wherever possible to the indicators of key drivers and other factors within the UK Government Strategy, except that they are not necessarily applicable across the whole of the UK.

Further developments on indicators

There was some support among consultees for aggregated indices, and in particular an 'ecological footprint' indicator within the consultation responses. We appreciate that an ecological footprint, which some consider provides a measure of global impact, may have potential as a future communication tool, especially as the Welsh Assembly Government has already adopted it as an indicator. The UK Government has therefore commissioned research to establish whether an ecological footprint could be constructed for the UK that overcomes concerns regarding transparency, robustness and meaningfulness. We are in addition looking at means of estimating indirect carbon dioxide emissions, including those embodied in the production and transportation of our imports from abroad.

Ideally, we should also be able to produce indicators of our global impact – to ensure that progress at home is not at the expense of the wider world. However, establishing meaningful and reliable measures that encompass economic and social, as well as environmental impacts, is a considerable challenge, owing to data constraints and other practicalities. Work will continue in this area, in particular by international organisations such as the Organisation for Economic Co-operation and Development.

We will build on the current indicators within the UK Government Strategy, and establish some measures for international sustainable development. These will include:

> showing how the UK compares internationally by setting UK indicators against comparative trends in other countries

> reporting on indicators of global and EU trends, and

> exploring the feasibility of indicators to measure UK impacts overseas. This would be on a pilot basis, looking at specific countries and key sectors (like timber or mineral extraction).

Within the UK Framework and UK Government Strategy there are several indicators where it is not yet possible for us to be precise about how they will be measured. For some of these there is already work underway which should enable us to define the indicator, and start reporting on progress within a short period. In other cases, the indicators represent an aspiration for those issues we wish to monitor. It may take longer to define them properly and establish routine data collection – not least as the indicators need to be established within a well-defined policy context and in some cases the policy development is also at an early stage. For all the indicators to be developed, we will expand on what might be measured, and specify a timetable, as part of the first monitoring report on the UK Framework and UK Government Strategy Indicators.

In particular, the Departments for Environment Food and Rural Affairs (Defra), and for Education and Skills (DfES) are actively seeking to develop an indicator to show the impact of formal learning on knowledge and awareness of sustainable development. Further work is needed on this, but the Government hopes that a suitable indicator will be agreed later in 2005.

Environmental equality and social justice are key areas for which we may need to establish further indicators, and the recent Sustainable Development Research Network Environment and Social Justice Rapid Research and Evidence Review provides a useful foundation for further work.[3]

The 1999 Strategy contained a commitment to develop an indicator of wellbeing. In response to this commitment, Defra's 2001 survey of public attitudes to quality of life and to the environment in England (Defra 2002) asked a series of new questions about reported life-satisfaction. Further progress on this issue has been made by a Prime

---

[3] See www.sd-research.org.uk/documents/ESJ_final_report.pdf

Minister's Strategy Unit report on life-satisfaction and by more recent work on wellbeing in this country and elsewhere.[4] The issue of wellbeing lies at the heart of sustainable development, and it remains important to develop appropriate wellbeing indicators.

Many of our existing indicators cover issues that affect people's wellbeing, for example employment, community participation, education, housing conditions, health, income, and the environment more generally.

What is missing is a means of making sure that wellbeing issues are being tackled consistently, in the right way, and that we are genuinely making a difference to people's lives. Some appreciation of this may in part be provided by extending our indicators to include such issues as mental health, access to sport and culture, green space, neighbourliness, which we will explore.

> **In order to get a better understanding and focus on wellbeing, by the end of 2006 the Government will sponsor cross-disciplinary work to bring together existing research and international experience and to explore how policies might change with an explicit wellbeing focus**

Depending on the strength of the evidence base, such work could be used to inform future policy development and spending decisions, as this sustainable development strategy is implemented. It could also provide the basis for developing a more comprehensive set of wellbeing indicators to support the Framework and our separate sustainable development strategies.

---

[4] PM Strategy Unit, November 2002, 'Life-satisfaction: the state of knowledge and implications for government'; The World in 2005, The Economist, December 2004, 'The Economist Intelligence Unit's quality of life index'; Richard Layard, February 2005, 'Happiness: lessons from a new science'; New Economics Foundation, 2004,
'A Wellbeing Manifesto for a Flourishing Society'; Australian Centre on Quality of Life, August 2004, 'Australian Unity Wellbeing Index'.

Chapter 2
Helping People Make Better Choices

The facts

> 30% of people claim to care about companies' environmental and social record; but only 3% reflect this in their purchases[1]

> Whilst 90% of people know that drinks cans can be recycled, only 50% say they have actually ever done it[2]

> *"The Government leading by example will have a galvanizing effect for other sectors"* (consultation response to 'Taking it on', KPMG, 2004)

> 60% of Britons think that global warming would be best tackled at a global level. Just under 1 in 10 people (9%) think it would be best tackled by individual households[3]

> Cycling in London has risen by 30% since the introduction of the congestion charge[4]

[1] Co-Op Bank, 2000
[2] NOP World research for WRAP, 2004
[3] BBC/ICM, July 2004, poll on climate change, at http://news.bbc.co.uk/nol/shared/bsp/hi/pdfs/ 28_07_04_climatepoll.pdf
[4] www.dft.gov.uk

Summary

Behaviour changes will be needed to deliver sustainable development. However, attitude and behaviour change is a complex subject. Information alone does not lead to behaviour change or close the so-called "attitude-behaviour gap". This chapter introduces a comprehensive behaviour change model for policy making, which will be applied in all priority areas. One of the key elements of the new approach is the need to engage people close to home. The new Community Action 2020 – Together We Can programme, to be launched later this year will support communities to work together to make the world more sustainable for themselves and future generations.

Taking it on consultation responses

The majority of respondents recognised the importance of education, information, taxation, regulations, media campaigns and Government leadership as ways of changing behaviour. However, a few responses noted the limitations of these approaches when used individually, stating that they worked better as a package of measures tackling a variety of barriers at once.

1. Our approach

We all – governments, businesses, families and communities, the public sector, voluntary and community organisations – need to make different choices if we are to achieve the vision of sustainable development. What we have done in the past has led to some significant changes but failed to make that fundamental shift. In this chapter we propose a new approach based on research[5] on what influences the way we choose now. This brings together the levers that we have and gives greater recognition to some of the social and practical factors that influence and limit our choices – and recognises that we need a much more active approach to change habits.

> *"Information does not necessarily lead to increased awareness, and increased awareness does not necessarily lead to action. Information provision, whether through advertisements, leaflets or labelling, must be backed up by other approaches."*
>
> **Demos & Green Alliance, 2003**

Traditional regulation has been a driver of higher environmental standards and rising levels of social protection. It will continue to have a role to play. The Government's approach to regulation means looking for alternatives to "classic" command and control regulation – through advice, voluntary agreements and use of economic instruments – such as taxes or trading schemes. Where regulation

5 ▸ Jackson, T, 2005. 'Motivating Sustainable Consumption – a review of evidence on consumer behaviour and behavioural change' at www.sd-research.org.uk/documents/ MotivatingSCfinal.pdf

▸ Andrew Darnton, for Defra, March 2004, 'The impact of sustainable development on public behaviour' at www.sustainable-development.gov.uk (publications page)

▸ Andrew Darnton, for Defra, May 2004, 'Driving public behaviours for sustainable lifestyles' at www.sustainable-development.gov.uk (publications page)

▸ Prime Minister Strategy Unit, February 2004, 'Personal Responsibility and Changing Behaviour: the state of knowledge and its implications for public policy' at www.number10.gov.uk/files/pdf/pr.pdf

▸ Demos and the Green Alliance, for Defra, December 2003, 'Carrots, sticks and sermons: influencing public behaviour for environmental goals' at www.green-alliance.org.uk/publications/PubCarrotsSticksSermons/

remains the best option, the best results will be delivered through regulations which are focused on outcomes and are backed up by clear information and consistent enforcement[6].

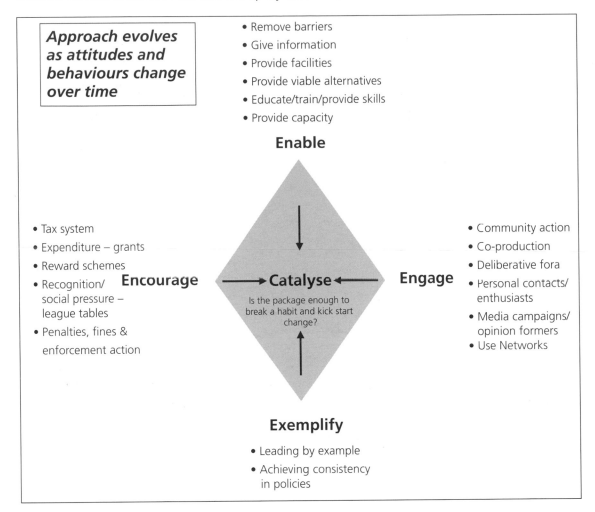

Approach evolves as attitudes and behaviours change over time

- Remove barriers
- Give information
- Provide facilities
- Provide viable alternatives
- Educate/train/provide skills
- Provide capacity

Enable

- Tax system
- Expenditure – grants
- Reward schemes
- Recognition/ social pressure – league tables
- Penalties, fines & enforcement action

Encourage

Catalyse
Is the package enough to break a habit and kick start change?

Engage

- Community action
- Co-production
- Deliberative fora
- Personal contacts/ enthusiasts
- Media campaigns/ opinion formers
- Use Networks

Exemplify

- Leading by example
- Achieving consistency in policies

While there will continue to be a very important role for regulation and enforcement, regulation alone will not be able to deliver the changes we want to see. We need to make sure that we are using the levers available in a consistent way. The new strategy therefore focuses on the need to **enable, encourage and engage** people and communities in the move toward sustainability; recognising that Government needs **to lead by example**. The diagram above sets out what the elements under each of these headings could comprise.

A cyclist enters London's congestion charge zone

While these elements are all necessary for change to take place they may not be sufficient to bring about the changes we need when behaviour is entrenched. In these circumstances, we may need to go further and think about how we design policies to **catalyse** people to behave differently. Over time the aim is for the new behaviour to become the norm. That in turn can open up further possibilities for progress.

London's congestion charge provides an example of how this model can work in practice. A combination of charging, combined with increased provision of buses was introduced with a huge amount of accompanying publicity. It has had effects that have been far greater

---

6 The Better Regulation Task Force was established in September 1997. It is an independent body that advises Government on action to ensure that regulation and its enforcement accord with the five Principles of Good Regulation: Proportionality; Accountability; Consistency; Transparency; Targeting.

than originally forecast. There has been a 30 per cent reduction in congestion as people consider alternatives including public transport with an increase of 29,000 bus passengers entering the zone in the morning peak.

Government recognises the need for a comprehensive and consistent approach if we are to change deep-seated habits[7]. We have applied this approach across the priority areas set out in following chapters. This is key to delivering sustainable development, but there are synergies with many other areas – for example, the emphasis on healthier lifestyles in the Public Health White paper or the Home Office's agenda on civic renewal.

There is also a lot of innovative activity going on at local level and through programmes funded by the Government's Environmental Action Fund.

A three-year project, **ChangeLAB – Changing Lifestyles, Attitudes and Behaviour –** creates a European-wide knowledge base about effective local interventions to influence behaviour in sustainable directions, particularly regarding waste, transport, energy and water use. Funded under the EU's Interreg IIIC programme and led by Surrey County Council, ChangeLAB involves eight partners from Member States.

➤ **In order to evaluate and share what works best in practice we are establishing a "behaviour change" forum across Government departments and other stakeholders. This will enable behaviour change to be better understood among policy makers; help behaviour-based policies to be more successful through greater policy coherence and evaluation; and promote understanding of behaviour change as a core policy skill.**

➤ **To share information and to help people help us take forward the new strategy Government sustainable development website: www.sustainable-development.gov.uk is being re-launched. This will be developed into a resource centre for those who want to take action to deliver sustainable development.**

The rest of this chapter sets out more detail on the tools and approaches we will use. In the chapters on the priorities we show how we will apply this integrated approach in practice.

2. Community Action 2020 – Together We Can

Action by citizens and communities is central to the implementation of this new approach. Government has already recognised this in its broader commitment to community engagement.

The World Summit on Sustainable Development, in 2002, called for a greater emphasis on action. And one of the messages of the research is that sustainable development often works best when driven by people working together. We can learn and change our behaviour more effectively in groups: Community groups can help tackle climate change, develop community energy and transport projects, help minimise waste, improve the quality of the local environment, and promote fair trade and sustainable consumption and production.

---

[7] A more detailed paper on the changing behaviour model is available on the Governments sustainable development website – www.sustainable-development.gov.uk

The Home Office review of capacity building found that communities often do not have the skills or confidence to get involved and often do not have the support they need within easy reach. Better co-ordination is also needed within the voluntary and community sector and between national and local levels. Government's priorities for action in light of the review are set out in 'Firm Foundations: the Government's framework for community capacity building' (Home Office, 2004).

'Taking it on' responses supported the Home Office findings:

▶ "Sustainable development was not well understood by the community" (Focus Group)

▶ Communities need "more support from the local and county council" (Residents Association)

▶ One Environmental Forum wanted "community action groups and other interested parties to have a bigger say on council strategies", and

▶ The Regional Report from North East commented that there is "a lot of good work on sustainable development by local authorities through their development of Local Agenda 21 strategies."

"We are social creatures, our behaviours are shaped and constrained by social norms and expectations. Negotiating change is best pursued at the level of groups and communities. Social support is particularly vital in breaking habits, and in devising new social norms and more sustainable patterns of consumption. Government can play a vital role in nurturing and supporting community based social change."

Motivating Sustainable Consumption, Professor Tim Jackson, University of Surrey

In England, a cross-government action plan, '**Together We Can**' is being developed to increase community engagement in solving public problems and improving people's quality of life. Led by the Home Office, the action plan draws together activities across a wide range of public policies and will set out specific areas where people will be given support to engage more with the work of public bodies so that together they can:

▶ build safer communities

▶ reduce re-offending and raise confidence in the criminal justice system

▶ support young people's development

▶ increase community cohesion, intergenerational activity and race equality

▶ strengthen democracy

▶ revitalise neighbourhoods

▶ make the best use of schools, and

▶ improve public health.

This Sustainable Development Strategy shares the same interest in involving more people in achieving its goals as other policy areas in the Together We Can action plan. This common interest is to be taken forward by a new programme to be called **Community Action 2020 – Together We Can**. This will form a key strand in the Together We Can action plan. It builds upon experience gained from Local Agenda 21, launched at the Rio Summit 1992, which inspired communities across the UK which is still being pursued in some areas, and has delivered real benefits. The message from the consultation however was that Government needed to re-energise community action to achieve a step change in the delivery of sustainable development[8].

Community Action 2020 – Together We Can is a programme of support for community action on sustainable development, implementing the Prime Minister's call for action.

Thousands of community groups are already making a massive contribution to improving quality of life in their area. By thinking globally and acting locally, together, we can make a huge difference – to our neighbourhoods, our quality of life, and the future of our children. In today's world, small individual actions can add up to big changes for the better at the national and even international level.

"Many local communities understand the links between the need to tackle national and global environmental challenges and everyday actions to improve our neighbourhoods and create better places to live. In 1997 I encouraged all local authorities to work with communities and produce Local Agenda 21 plans by 2000. There was an overwhelming response: from County Durham to Wiltshire and from Redbridge to Cheshire, local people showed what could be done. Next year, as a key part of our new Sustainable Development Strategy, I want to reinvigorate community action on sustainable development."

Rt. Hon. Tony Blair MP, Prime Minister – 14th September 2004

> **The Government will launch Community Action 2020 – Together We Can later in 2005 as a catalyst for thinking globally and acting locally in communities across England**

Community Action 2020 – Together We Can will re-invigorate community action on sustainable development by promoting new and existing opportunities to get involved in action of this kind. It will set out what is to be done to enable, encourage, engage and exemplify community action to increase sustainability and contribute to the priorities set out in subsequent chapters of this strategy.

---

[8] A Joseph Rowntree Foundation report: Church and Elster, JRF, 2002, 'Thinking locally, acting nationally', found that in response to Local Agenda 21 (LA 21):
> Over 400 programmes took root across the UK.
> These programmes had a significant collective impact on targets for sustainable development, but this could grow more if more support was available to remove barriers to action.

Community workers helped promote environmental activity but lacked information on what works. Many LA21 programmes have struggled to recruit deprived and excluded communities, black and minority ethnic groups and younger and older sections of the population. Karen Lucas, Andrew Ross and Sara Fuller, JRF 2003, 'What's in a name? Local Agenda 21, community planning and neighbourhood renewal'.

**Community Action 2020 –
Together We Can**

- Strengthen the capacity of **Community Mentors and Community Development Workers** to support community action on sustainable development
- Increase **learning opportunities and training on sustainable development**
- Improve **access to seedcorn funding** for community projects on sustainable development
- Forge links with the **schools citizenship and sustainable development syllabuses**
- Improve **information of funding** availability

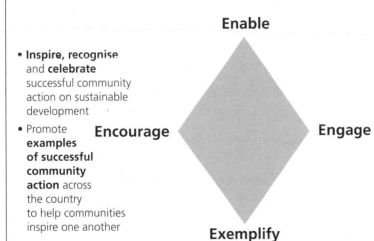

Enable

- **Inspire, recognise** and **celebrate** successful community action on sustainable development
- Promote **examples of successful community action** across the country to help communities inspire one another

Encourage

Engage

- **Provide opportunities for community involvement** in Sustainable Community Strategies and local action plans such as parish plans, neighbourhood plans, housing and planning policies
- Improve the promotion of **volunteering opportunities** on sustainable development
- **Build links** to improve opportunities for action through existing initiatives

Exemplify

- Lead by example with **clear and consistent messages** from central government on community empowerment and sustainable development through:
  - Vision for Sustainable Communities (Chapter 6)
  - Departments will support **employee volunteering schemes**

Community Action 2020 – Together We Can will enable community development practitioners and mentors to be better equipped to support communities. The Government will work with key stakeholders in the community sector to achieve this by:

➤ **improving access to information, advice, materials, community packs, web portals and training which will all help communities take action on sustainable development**

➤ **increasing opportunities for community workers and communities to learn about sustainable development**

➤ **including sustainable development in National Occupational Standards and accredited units which set out the skills and principles of practice for community development work, and**

> **increasing opportunities for individuals within communities to volunteer in sustainable development activity.**

Community Action 2020 – Together We Can will encourage the recognition and valuing of communities' efforts:

> by raising awareness of community awards and providing more information about them, and

> by improving access to sources of funding for environmental and sustainable development projects[9].

The Big Lottery Fund

The Big Lottery Fund is the merged organisation of the New Opportunities Fund and the Community Fund. It supports charities and the voluntary sector and health, education and the environment and has taken on the Millennium Commission's responsibilities for funding large-scale regenerative projects.

Big Lottery Fund is working with the Sustainable Development Commission to deliver on the commitment to sustainable development set out in the 2003 statement by the New Opportunities Fund. This work will consider how the funding application, assessment and evaluation process could be improved in terms of its potential to deliver sustainable development.

The Big Lottery Fund has also requested support around the development of their new funding priorities and their forthcoming transformational grants programme, to ensure that they have incorporated sustainability principles.

There are already many examples of community projects, which help contribute to achieving sustainable development in the UK. By showing what can be achieved by small community groups, others gain in confidence. Sharing success stories can motivate and inspire people to make things happen in their own community. So Community Action 2020 – Together We Can will promote the exchange of information and experience between successful community projects and other communities who want to learn through training and web-based dissemination of good practice.

In partnership with local government and other local public bodies, it will engage people in planning for the future of their local neighbourhoods or parishes[10] and influencing the delivery of services in their area.

The Government appreciates the work of voluntary and community organisations in enabling individuals to contribute to the development of their communities. The Government is committed to working in partnership

Communities 'Taking it on' in the public consultation for the Strategy review

---

[9] The Home Office online portal (www.governmentfunding.org.uk) provides access to grants for the voluntary and community sectors

[10] In Chapter 6 we describe how communities should be involved in drawing up plans which affect them: the Government will support local authorities to do more to engage communities.

with the voluntary and community sector through the principles of the Compact on Relations between Government and the Voluntary and Community Sector[11].

Government as an employer can lead by example by supporting employees who volunteer for their community. The Department for Environment, Food and Rural Affairs (Defra), the Home Office and the Department for Education and Skills already do so.

3. A new approach to communications and engagement

Evaluation of past awareness raising campaigns suggests that they have raised awareness but not translated into action. The new approach to climate change communications, launched in February 2005, is designed to address some of the past inadequacies. It will contribute to Community Action 2020 – Together We Can and help engage wider community action at the local level.

The toolkit for climate change communications (see Chapter 4) is designed to provide a model for future behaviour change campaigns on other issues. Key components of the initiative are:

> using positive and inspirational messages rather than fear or concern

> avoiding 'above the line' advertising e.g. TV or billboard

> galvanising local and regional communicators for climate change through financial support and guidance

> high-profile national communications to support the local and regional initiatives, and

> developing a new inspirational goal and a branded statement are recommended to link the communications of different organisations.

The effectiveness of this new initiative will be evaluated and used to improve the approach going forward.

---

[11] More details under www.thecompact.org.uk.

The London 2012 Olympic bid: Making sustainable development real...

All our evidence shows that people find it difficult to relate to the general concept of sustainable development. We need therefore to exploit opportunities to show the benefits of sustainable development through things that people are interested in and do relate to.

Sustainability is a hallmark of London's Olympic bid. As well as being a key selling point for the London bid to the International Olympic Committee, it offers a unique, very high profile way of communicating the benefits of a sustainable approach to a wider public who would turn to the off switch if lectured on sustainable development.

Proposed Olympic Park London 2012

London 2012 is working closely with WWF-UK and Bioregional, a local charity, to introduce the concept of a 'One Planet Olympics'[12]. This introduces the sense of a more equitable share of finite resources, which complements the Olympic ideal of "sport and the harmonious development of mankind".

Sustainability goals for the London Olympic bid include:

❯ low carbon Games – to reduce energy demand and meet it from zero/low carbon and renewable sources and to showcase how the Olympic Games are adapting to a world increasingly affected by climate change

❯ zero waste Games – to avoid landfill by reducing waste at source, then reusing, recycling and recovering all remaining waste

❯ conservation of biodiversity – to conserve natural habitats and wildlife, improve the quality of urban greenspace and to bring nature closer to people

❯ sustainable transport – to reduce the need for travel and provide sustainable alternatives to the private car, and

❯ sustainable legacy – to promote health and wellbeing through an integrated package of sporting, environmental and cultural initiatives.

Work by the Prime Minister's Strategy Unit[13] suggests that involving people directly in policy design may lead to more successful outcomes. There have already been some experiments with deliberative fora and citizens' juries where representative citizens help governments develop policy. These allow more in-depth discussion about options than

[12] WWF, Bioregional, 2005, Towards a One Planet Olympics – Achieving the first sustainable Olympic Games and Paralympic Games. One Planet Living is a joint initiative between WWF and Bioregional.
[13] Prime Minister Strategy Unit, February 2004, 'Personal Responsibility and Changing Behaviour: the state of knowledge and its implications for public policy' at www.number10.gov.uk/files/pdf/pr.pdf

an opinion poll or focus group – and allow people to judge trade-offs based on evidence and opinion from advocates and experts. In Texas it led to a change in energy policy; the Department for Culture, Media and Sport used this approach for the BBC charter review and the Department of Trade and Industry had citizens juries on flexible working. Some local authorities have been using deliberative techniques to help resolve some of the difficult decisions around waste disposal and recycling.

Defra has run two pilot workshops on "sustainable lifestyles" to test the possibility of organising a large-scale deliberative forum to feed into policy development. Initial results appear promising and can be viewed on the Government's sustainable development website: www.sustainable-government.gov.uk.

> **The Government is joining forces with the Roundtable on Sustainable Consumption to design and run a "deliberative forum" in 2006 – a two-three day discussion between 100-200 people representative of the country as a whole. They will look at how Government and citizens can work together to move towards a "one planet economy", a concept discussed in Chapter 3**

We will also want to involve stakeholders directly in taking this strategy forward. This will help to keep the Strategy as a living document and allow it to be updated as we learn more, or need to respond to new issues.

> **From the end of 2005 we will pilot open and innovative ways to enable stakeholders to influence decisions about the kind of projects, which would deliver the goals of this strategy**

4. Using incentives

Incentives can take a number of forms including subsidies, voluntary initiatives, trading schemes or taxes. The reasons for using incentives can be to correct externalities or market failures – where the private costs do not reflect the real cost – or as a way of changing behaviours to achieve particular targets. Changing behaviour through ensuring we give the right price signals can be a very effective way of delivering our objectives at least cost to the economy.

The Government's thinking on using economic instruments to tackle environmental issues were most recently set out in 'Tax and the Environment: using economic instruments' (HM Treasury 2002).

This document sets out the key principles that Government will apply when determining whether there is a role for economic instruments to tackle particular environmental issues. Environmental taxes are fundamentally different to most other taxes; their principal aim is to deliver more efficient and better environmental outcomes, not necessarily to raise revenue. So the way in which environmental taxes should be applied is also different. In particular, in developing policy on environmental taxation, attention is paid to:

> advance notice of new environmental taxes with extensive consultation on its design to allow people or firms to adapt their practices – for example, with the Climate Change Levy

> recycling some of the proceeds back to the sector paying the tax to help speed the response

> allow discounts in tax levels in return for negotiated commitments to reduce pollution, and

> using some of the proceeds to offer alternatives.

In other cases, taxes might not be the right choice and better results can be achieved through regulation (where for example we need to control local pollution impacts), trading schemes or voluntary agreements. Often the best approach will involve a package of measures, which could include some market incentives such as, for example, emissions trading or the Renewables Obligation. In all cases our aim must be to apply these measures in a sustainable way. That means:

> being clear about the environmental benefits we want to achieve

> choosing the measure that will impose least economic cost and most potential for economic benefit (for example, encouraging innovation)

> making sure that the change is fair and in particular that vulnerable groups do not bear too high a burden, and

> ensuring a degree of public acceptance.

Using incentives – road pricing

Road pricing or road user charging is designed to influence the behaviour of road users, to encourage them to avoid driving at busy times and places in order to allow traffic to flow more freely.

The Government welcomed the findings of the road pricing feasibility study[14], which found that a carefully constructed road pricing scheme could make a valuable contribution to reducing the environmental impacts of roads and traffic as well as its prime objective of managing traffic to reduce congestion.

The study found that a carefully constructed scheme could help to reduce greenhouse gas emissions as well as help with more localised emissions, but the impact is not entirely clear cut and would depend on the precise nature of the scheme. The Government agrees that the time has come to consider seriously the role that could be played by some form of road pricing policy and will look carefully at potential environmental impacts as work on road pricing is taken forward, alongside the potential benefits arising from other measures to improve the management and use of the road network.

The Government continues to refine its approach to the use of economic instruments. Particular methodological and analytical issues, which have been kept under review, include:

> improving the links between environmental impacts and economic growth, particularly the challenge to global growth from climate change

> getting the right balance of environmental tax, other economic instruments and other policy interventions, in particular the role of price and quantity based economic instruments

14 www.dft.gov.uk/stellent/groups/dft_roads/documents/divisionhomepage/029709.hcsp

▶ the role of economic instruments in encouraging innovation and new technologies

▶ intervening at the points where it is likely to have most impact, for example getting the right balance between incentivising waste minimisation and recycling

▶ using combinations of different policy interventions, such as regulation tied to trading

▶ taking account of some of the wider effects of using economic instruments, such as the behavioural change that results from making announcements about the implementation of policy

▶ interventions will not be used in isolation but will be allied with education and communication, and

▶ ongoing evaluation of the impacts of measures and taking account of these lessons.

▶ **To advance understanding on the role of economic instruments evaluations of the Climate Change Levy and Aggregates Levy are underway. The results of these evaluations will help to build a more comprehensive picture of the effectiveness of environmental taxes and will inform other reviews, including that of the Climate Change Programme and a further stocktake of the evaluation of environmental tax policy for the Budget.**

Examples of Interventions

Tax	Trading scheme	Mixed Instruments	Tax credits/ public spending	Voluntary agreements
Landfill Tax Escalator (standard tax rate to increase annually by £3 from April 2005 to reach a medium/ long term rate of £35 per tonne. New lower rate of Vehicle Excise Duty for the most environmentally friendly cars.	EU Emissions Trading Scheme January 2005. Landfill Allowance Trading Scheme, April 2005.	Renewables Obligation – a mixed instrument comprising a regulation and trading of renewable obligation certificates. Inland Revenue rules encourage employees to cycle to work in a number of ways including tax-efficient bike purchase from salary.	Recycling of revenues from Landfill Tax Escalator to business.	The Pesticides Voluntary Initiative was accepted by the Government on the 1st April 2001, in place of a proposed tax on pesticides used in agriculture and horticulture. The Ethical Trading Initiative (ETI) is an organisation comprising corporations, NGOs, and Trade Unions which is committed to improving the conditions of workers in the global supply chains of corporate members through voluntary agreements and codes of conduct.

The tax system works at national level – but in many cases we want more targeted incentives. Recent work has focused on local or targeted "positive incentives"[15] in motivating more sustainable behaviour. We will consider the scope for using such incentives.

[15] Maxine Holdsworth and David Boyle, National Consumer Council, 2004, 'Carrots not sticks: the possibilities of a sustainable consumption reward card for the UK' at www.ncc.org.uk

5. Forming habits early – the role of education

Formal education has a crucial role to play in both raising awareness among young people of sustainable development, giving them the skills they need to put sustainable development into practice in later life; but also in forming good habits at an early age.

"The people who will succeed fifteen years from now, the countries which will succeed, are those which are most based on a sustainable vision of the world. That is what we should be training people to do."

Rt. Hon. Charles Clarke MP, Secretary of State for Education and Skills, 2003

Sustainable development principles must lie at the core of the education system, such that schools, colleges and universities become showcases of sustainable development among the communities that they serve.

There is a two way benefit from embedding sustainable development in the education system. By linking teaching to issues of direct concern to young people – their personal quality of life, and the wellbeing of the communities and environment around them – their learning becomes more relevant and compelling, with positive impacts on standards of achievement and behaviour. Working towards sustainable development goals can also increase the sense of purpose felt by staff in schools, colleges and universities, with impacts on morale, retention and recruitment of new staff.

On behalf of the Government, the Department for Education and Skills (DfES) aims to ensure that sustainable development is embedded in the core education agenda across all education and skills sectors. A Sustainable Development Action Plan for Education and Skills, was launched in September 2003.

Schools

The DfES' Five Year Strategy for Children and Learners contains a vision that:

'Every school should (also) be an environmentally sustainable school, with a good plan for school transport that encourages walking and cycling, an active and effective recycling policy (moving from paper to electronic processes wherever possible) and a school garden or other opportunities for children to explore the natural world. Schools must teach our children by example as well as instruction.'

There is an opportunity for schools to develop the skills of sustainable living not just through the curriculum, but through the examples that teachers set on a daily basis, and through pupils' direct experience of living and studying within the school environment. Through parents and other sections of the local community, good habits established in young people have the potential to exert influence far beyond the classroom. We are keen to give further encouragement to teenagers – often the group with the highest levels of interest in the environment but least likely to translate that into action – to put their beliefs into action.

"The Government is now developing a school specific method of environmental assessment that will apply to all new school buildings. Sustainable development will not just be a subject in the classroom: it will be in its bricks and mortar and the way the school uses and even generates its own power. Our students won't just be told about sustainable development, they will see and work within it: a living, learning place in which to explore what a sustainable lifestyle means."

Rt. Hon. Tony Blair MP, Prime Minister
14th September 2004

Source: DfES

> **Defra and the Connexions Card Service of the DfES are launching a joint pilot initiative in schools and colleges to reward student behaviour – individual or in a group – which recognises and responds to environmental and community issues**

Through the Extended Schools initiative, we are exploring ways in which schools can actively support sustainable development in their local communities, leading to practical improvements in local quality of life. Good examples are school transport, where the Government is promoting healthier, greener and safer ways of travelling to school, and healthy living, where projects to improve school food and reinforce healthy eating messages in the classroom are underway.

As far as the curriculum is concerned, the Government is working to build capacity within subjects such as citizenship, geography, religious education and science. These subjects are already used to explore sustainable development in various contexts, helping pupils to grow into responsible decision-makers and informed problem-solvers. We want to make it easier for teachers and school leaders to make their schools more environmentally friendly and sustainable.

Children exploring nature through a wildlife pond at Greenwich Millennium Primary School

> **In 2005 the Government will launch a sustainable development framework for schools, a web-based service hosted within www.teachernet.gov.uk, providing a one-stop shop for teachers and school leaders**

Over the next 10-15 years, the Government is committed to renewing all secondary schools (currently, some 3,400), in particular through the **Building Schools for the Future** programme. All new schools will need to be rated 'very good' according to a system designed with the Building Research Establishment.

Life-long sustainable development

The good work started in schools needs to be continued on into higher education and professional development.

> **The Learning and Skills Council (LSC) and Higher Education Funding Council for England (HEFCE) will publish their own strategies for sustainable development later in 2005**

The strategies, which are being developed following extensive processes of consultation, aim to encourage institutions within the college and university sectors to embed sustainable development within their teaching and learning, their management and leadership, and their engagement with the wider community.

To maintain a more competitive economy, to compete internationally and build ourselves sustainable communities, we need to improve the knowledge and skills base of everyone, including professionals and others in the workplace. Later parts of the strategy set out how we are planning to upgrade public sector skills for sustainable development, help business with corporate social responsibility and develop a strategy for sustainable development in the workplace, but we need to make "sustainability literacy" a core competency for professional graduates.

DD, the mascot for the UNESCO ESD website

▶ **DfES is working with Forum for the Future to ensure sustainability is promoted across the spectrum of professional bodies**

The Government will implement the United Nations Strategy for Education for Sustainable Development (ESD), which underpins the UN Decade for ESD running from 2005-2014, and will seek ways in which to help other countries develop their own sustainable development education strategies.

DfES launched the Global Gateway in February 2004[16]. Working with British Council International, the website enables people involved in education across the world to engage in creative partnerships. This will help to ensure that education crosses national boundaries and that young people become truly global citizens.

---

[16] www.globalgateway.org.uk/

Skills for Sustainable Development

DfES have done much to **embed sustainable development into the school curriculum**, and their Sustainable Development Action Plan commits them to embedding sustainable development in all areas.

DfES is also keen that **"Sustainability Literacy"** becomes a core competency for **professional graduates**. DfES has, with Forum for the Future and professional organisations, set up the **Sustainability Integration group** to raise the profile of sustainability literacy in the professional curricula.

Sustainable development will be embedded into the **curriculum of the National School of Government**, in areas such as policy making, strategic leadership, programme and project management and the behavioural aspects of management development.

This will build on current workshops with senior civil servants on sustainable development run by the Centre for Management and Policy Studies.

The Government will work to increase the range of learning opportunities on sustainable development available to all **community practitioners.**

It will expand the **National Occupational Standards** to include Sustainable Communities and explore developing an additional accredited unit.

Community Action 2020 – Together We Can will enhance the skills of community groups in sustainable development to be able to participate in discussions with local Government and leaders of Local Strategic Partnerships.

During 2005 the Government will establish a new **Academy for Sustainable Communities** which will work together with partners to develop sustainable development learning opportunities for Local Strategic Partnerships as well as **Sir John Egan's core occupations** as set out in his review of sustainable community skills.

The launch of a **new Government Corporate Social Responsibility (CSR) website** outlining Government support for CSR, with links to other CSR organisations and case studies of best practice.

The establishing of a **CSR Academy** to support skills development in this area.

Sustainable development competencies are **integrated into all the main professional bodies**, including their registration requirements and qualifications.

During 2005, the Improvement and Development Agency (IDeA) will roll out a **Sustainable Communities module** within the **Leadership Academy** to build the capacity of **local authority Leaders** and **Chief Executives**.

A **peer review toolkit** on sustainable communities will also be launched.

We will work through the Centres of Excellence to encourage **sustainable procurement** throughout **local government and improved skills training:**

As part of the **Future Leadership programme** for local authority middle managers, we will introduce material to improve **awareness and understanding** about delivering sustainable communities.

Chapter 3
"One Planet Economy": Sustainable Consumption and Production

The facts

> By 2050, global energy demand could double as populations rise and developing countries expand their economies[1]

> Since 1950, global water use has more than tripled; within 25 years, half the world's population could have trouble finding enough freshwater for drinking and irrigation[2]

> The cost of wasted natural resources to UK manufacturing industry is equivalent to around 7% of profit[3], and energy efficiency improvements by business and individuals could save £12 billion annually across the UK economy[4]

> Production, distribution and consumption of food in the UK is responsible for around 22% of its total greenhouse gas emissions – other significant sources are heating, lighting and domestic appliances, private transport and air travel[5]

> More than 80% of all product-related environmental impacts are determined by product design[6]

> New fridge freezers sold in the UK today consume on average 50% less energy than those sold just 8 years ago[7]

[1] World Energy Organisation at www.worldenergy.org/wec-geis/edc/scenario.asp
[2] United Nations Environment Programme, 2003, Key facts, at www.unep.org/wed/2003/keyfacts.htm
[3] Cambridge Econometrics and AEA Technology for the Environment Agency, 'The benefits of Greener Business', at www.environment-agency.gov.uk/business/
[4] 'The Energy Review – performance and innovation unit report', at www.number-10.gov.uk/su/energy/1.html
[5] e2 Consulting, Bourne 2002 and Office of National Statistics, 2004, 'Achieving the UK's climate change commitments: the efficiency of the food cycle'.
[6] German Federal Environment Agency (ed), 2000, 'How to do ecodesign: A guide for environmentally friendly and economically sound design'.
[7] Market Transformation Programme at www.mtprog.com

Summary

Increasing prosperity, in the UK and across the world, has allowed many people to enjoy the benefits of goods and services which were once available to just a few. Nevertheless, the environmental impacts from our consumption and production patterns remain severe, and inefficient use of resources is a drag on the UK's economy and business. We need a major shift to deliver new products and services with lower environmental impacts across their life cycle, while at the same time boosting competitiveness. And we need to build on people's growing awareness of social and environmental concerns, and the importance of their roles as citizens and consumers.

Taking it on consultation responses

Responses to questions on Sustainable Consumption and Production (SCP) and on the business contribution to sustainable development fell into two broad categories of (i) better education and awareness and (ii) the use of both 'carrots and sticks' for business and consumers.

For example, there were calls for: better consumer information and labelling; the use of economic incentives/disincentives; better regulation; increased environmental reporting; tackling issues related to products, services and consumption as well as production; Government leadership (particularly in its procurement); identifying clear priorities for business to tackle.

Responses also highlighted key areas of consumption thought to be a priority: energy and fuel; transport/infrastructure; food; waste and packaging; resource use; and aviation.

1. The vision and challenge: "A one planet economy"

Sustainable consumption and production requires us to achieve more with less. Current developed country patterns of consumption and production could not be replicated world-wide: some calculations suggest that this could require three planets' worth of resources[8].

The largest and fastest growing pressures on the global environment come from areas such as household energy and water consumption, food consumption, travel and tourism. Past environmental policy focused mainly on pollution from domestic production activities. We now need a wider and more developed approach that focuses across the whole life cycle of goods, services and materials, also includes economic and social impacts, and in particular encompasses impacts outside the UK. There would be little value in reducing environmental impacts within the UK if the result were merely to displace those impacts overseas, or close off benefits at home or abroad.

The 1999 strategy's chapter on a sustainable economy reflected this approach. Since then, the 2002 World Summit on Sustainable Development (WSSD) set new global commitments on sustainable consumption and production. The Government followed this up with its own framework on sustainable consumption and production, 'Changing Patterns'[9]. This strategy now sets out how we are taking this forward, through measures to promote:

[8] World Wildlife Fund (WWF), 2004, 'Living Planet Report' at
www.panda.org/news_facts/publications/general/livingplanet/index.cfm

[9] Defra, 2003, 'Changing Patterns:' 'UK Government Framework for Sustainable Consumption and Production' at
www.defra.gov.uk/environment/business/scp/index.htm

➤ better products and services, which reduce the environmental impacts from the use of energy, resources, or hazardous substances

➤ cleaner, more efficient production processes, which strengthen competitiveness, and

➤ shifts in consumption towards goods and services with lower impacts.

➤ **The Government will continue to develop its policies on sustainable consumption and production, and will produce, by the end of 2006, a report on progress together with an updated plan of action in this area**

Success will involve tackling complex factors which affect consumption and production patterns. Social and cultural values lie behind people's aspirations and choices. Manufacturers and retailers have a major influence on both consumers and supply chains. Individual actions are often determined by local infrastructure, such as housing or transport links. Change will require innovation in both technologies and behaviours. Both Government and business have a responsibility to enable consumers to make sustainable choices.

Innovation for a sustainable future

The Government's 2003 innovation review identified the environment as a key driver for future innovation. Improved, lower impact products and services need to be developed. Some will be specific environmental goods and services, such as technologies to minimise pollutants or promote resource efficiency, or renewable energy sources. These already have a global market worth over $500 billion, but the scope for innovation extends far wider. For example, new materials, energy technologies and product design to minimise waste will all be important in future. Well designed environmental policy, with clear, long-term targets, can promote innovation and business opportunity.

Measures to stimulate this innovation will include:

➤ integrating sustainable development throughout the Department for Trade and Industry's (DTI) technology strategy, with funding of £150 million over the next 3 years for technologies critical to the future of the UK economy. For example, with up to £2 million support for a Resource Efficiency and Waste Knowledge Transfer Network offering a UK gateway for information and expertise and a focal point for business, government and academia to come together and provide integrated solutions

➤ playing a leading role in the EU's environmental technologies action plan

➤ using public procurement to build markets for new products and services and

➤ horizon scanning to identify trends and indicators of emerging innovations.

The review also launched a series of pilot projects on environmental regulation and innovation. These show that well-designed regulation, based on long term environmental objectives, can promote innovation and business opportunity.

These results will be used in a guide for policy-makers on 'Think Innovation', and the Government will also be holding a government/business workshop later this year on environmental regulation policy and its links to innovation.

An international vision

Our vision depends on international co-operation. Economic growth in both developed and developing countries drives trade in goods and services across the world in complex and fast-changing supply chains. For example, in the life cycle of a fridge or computer, extraction of raw materials, manufacturing, use and disposal may all occur in different countries. The Government therefore cannot make national policy in isolation. Yet international action touches on many difficult questions about development, trade, environment and global inequalities.

The Government will therefore press to strengthen:

> European Union (EU) efforts, by putting sustainable consumption and production at the heart of the new EU sustainable development strategy, and through a new thematic strategy on natural resources linked to action in key areas such as products, environmental technologies, commodities and public procurement.

> outcomes from the United Nations' 'Marrakech Process'[10], set up to take forward the World Summit on Sustainable Development[11] (WSSD) commitment on sustainable consumption and production. The UK is liaising with the United Nations Environment Programme (UNEP) and international partners to establish a technical task force to promote co-operation and improvements in sustainable products

> co-operation within the G8, by building on its '3Rs' (reduce, reuse, and recycle) initiative, to be hosted by the Japanese government in April 2005, and

> partnerships with major developing countries.

These efforts should lead to a clear EU programme for sustainable consumption and production, and the emergence of an international framework of programmes that can be agreed at the Commission on Sustainable Development in 2011 – CSD19. These are the prerequisites for the global delivery of the World Summit commitment on sustainable consumption and production.

Progress towards international goals is supported by policies in areas such as trade, agriculture, environment and technology. One of the objectives of the World Trade Organisation[12] (WTO) is to promote sustainable development and the Doha Development Agenda[13] calls for trade liberalisation, environmental protection and sustainable development to be mutually supportive.

[10] See www.un.org/esa/sustdev/sdissues/consumption/marratech.htm
[11] See www.un.org/events/wssd/
[12] See www.wto.org/
[13] See www.wto.org/english/tratop_e/dda_e/dda_e.htm

The Government will work with the EU through the WTO to:

> reduce unsustainable and environmentally damaging agriculture and fishing subsidies in the Doha Round

> promote the mutual supportiveness of trade liberalisation, environmental protection and sustainable development, for example by strengthening the links between WTO and those Multilateral Environmental Agreements that have trade provisions, and

> liberalise trade in environmental goods and services.

The Trade and Investment White Paper[14] deals more comprehensively with the question of how we can harnessthe power of globalisation, not only in the UK but in every country, especially in the developing world.

Children collecting floating waste from a polluted river in Manila Bay, Philippines
Source: Hartmut Schwarzbach/Unep/
Still pictures

A business vision

For business, sustainable consumption and production requires consideration of the implications for their business model together with their product and service range. Success will depend on their ability to meet growing consumer (household and supply-chain) expectations of higher environmental and ethical standards and to cut out the negative impacts of growing material resource consumption. Businesses that anticipate this trend and develop 'material light' goods and services will be best placed to benefit from these opportunities and to enhance their competitiveness.

This means that business' approach to corporate responsibility must extend throughout their supply-chains, from tackling the issues arising in the extraction of their raw materials, to engagement with consumers about the products and services they buy and eventually discard. But simply relying on consumers to make potentially complex choices is far from sufficient. Government therefore has a key role to play in developing the business case for sustainable consumption and production – for example through standards, economic incentives, regulation, voluntary agreements, business support programmes, communications and consumer policy. We set out below how the Government will take these forward, and will work closely with business in doing so.

In addition, we want to bring together a network of business expertise committed to working with Government to help us to make progress on consumption and production challenges together.

> **The Government will convene a new Sustainable Consumption and Production Business Task Force, which will be resourced to develop ideas for practical action on key aspects of sustainable consumption and production**

This Task Force will provide an important mechanism for building on the valuable work of the Advisory Committee on Business and the Environment[15] and the Advisory Committee on Consumer Products and the Environment[16], and will complement the work of the Round Table on Sustainable Consumption.

---

14 DTI, 2004, 'Trade and Investment White Paper 2004' at www.dti.gov.uk/ewt/whitepaper.htm
15 See www.defra.gov.uk/environment/acbe/default.htm
16 See www.defra.gov.uk/environment/consumerprod/accpe/index.htm

2. Sustainable Products – cutting out problems at source

We describe in Chapter 2 the challenge of influencing people to consider making more sustainable choices. But an equally big challenge is the fact that many of the avoidable impacts of what we buy are already 'designed-in', long before they are put into use.

The Government will therefore give much greater priority to a coherent 'product policy' approach through developing and publishing, by the end of 2006, a set of measures for taking forward integrated product policy, to:

➤ **reduce the environmental impacts of everyday products across their life cycle**

➤ **enhance measures to close the loop in the way we use resources (e.g. through recycling, re-use or remanufacturing)**

➤ **promote more radical new design solutions, which benefit the environment and the economy, and**

➤ **build up the knowledge and capacity needed to drive improvements in product markets.**

Raising product performance

The Government is expanding its Market Transformation Programme for sustainable products, putting in more resources and extending its scope beyond the current focus on energy and water impacts into the wider life cycle issues of key products, including chemicals, resource use and waste.

This will help to raise the game in using policy tools like public procurement specifications, minimum standards and publicly available information about the environmental performance of different products. It will also help to embed the 'environmental impact assessment' of products as a regular feature of good business practice.

'Thermafleece': Second Nature UK Ltd – winners of the 2004 Queen's Award for Enterprise in the sustainable development category, for its innovative insulation product
Source: Second Nature UK Ltd

Raising product standards

In a global market it is rarely feasible to set unilateral standards for traded goods. In most cases we must approach minimum standards, whether in law, through agreements made with industry or through negotiations at EU level.

There are some successes on which we can build. Mandatory standards to remove inefficient boilers and fridges from the market have been very effective (even the least efficient new fridge-freezer on sale today consumes only half as much energy as the least efficient products on the market eight years ago). The proposed framework directive for the Eco-design of Energy Using Products (the EUP Directive) will allow new standards to be set for any non-transport product that uses energy. Such measures could save around 10 per cent of total EU energy consumption by 2020. The Government will be seeking prompt agreement of this Directive, and will be considering whether its approach should be applied to non-energy product groups.

In parallel, EU-wide industry voluntary agreements have been negotiated with manufacturers to improve the energy performance of digital TV services, power supply units, televisions and DVD players; and to remove inefficient domestic washing machines and dishwashers from the market. We estimate that the digital TV services agreement alone has enabled the UK to head off additional carbon emissions of around 400000 tonnes a year.

Cutting-edge design for the environment

Better eco-design is crucial if we are to force the pace of improvements in product performance and stimulate real step changes. The Government can support this, first, by ensuring that relevant frameworks actively encourage better design – for example, public sector procurement and economic instruments will be used in ways which do not inhibit but actively reward innovation in producing lower-impact solutions. Secondly, the Government will promote eco-design as a mainstream element of good design practice.

▶ **The Government proposes to bring together expertise through a new Sustainable Design Forum to champion and educate in eco-design, and promote best practice tools and approaches which can be adopted by designers**

Minimising the effects of chemicals

Man-made chemicals are present in countless everyday products. Some 30,000 types of chemical are used in significant amounts, but we understand only a few hundred very well. The challenge the Government agreed at WSSD was to minimise the impacts of chemicals on health and the environment, and to help developing countries deal with the management of chemicals and hazardous wastes.

*Source: Martin Bond/
Still Pictures*

Our ability to meet this challenge will be strengthened by the new EU strategy on chemicals, known as REACH. We will continue to work hard to make sure REACH is effective and workable, so that it delivers a far better understanding of management, of chemicals in the environment and of their effects on human health.

Further measures will also be needed at the global level. We will push for early international adoption of an emerging agreement on a Strategic Approach to International Chemicals Management (SAICM).

The Government will also work with the chemical industry to assess the hazardous properties of chemicals and reduce the risk of harm to the environment where appropriate. Where chemicals have been shown to have persistent, bioaccumulative and toxic properties, the Government will encourage producers and users to substitute them with chemicals with less hazardous properties or to find alternative processes to meet the same requirement.

Building the capacity and frameworks for action on products

The Government's Advisory Committee on Consumer Products and the Environment (ACCPE) has put forward ideas for drawing together the strands of product knowledge and policy tools which are currently scattered across several departments, agencies and institutes. It has proposed establishing a new products agency, which would champion product sustainability, including running a knowledge base on products' environmental impacts, and helping retailers to assess the environmental impacts of their products.

❯ The Government will consult on ACCPE's ideas later in 2005

Building up information on product impacts is essential for the operation of the Environment Direct service that we describe in section 4. At the same time, at EU level, the Government will press for a more ambitious programme under the framework of Integrated Product Policy and for more targeted approaches like that of the draft Eco-design Framework Directive. Internationally, the Government will continue to work with governments in major trading blocks (such as China and the USA) on common priorities for cooperation on product standards and design. We will also work within UN structures to raise the profile of product standards and stimulate greater cooperation.

3. Sustainable Production – greater efficiency and value with less resource use, pollution and waste

Production processes have long been targeted by environmental legislation, with priority more recently on measures to tackle impacts such as carbon emissions and waste. Changes in the economy mean that we also need to address service industries as well as traditional manufacturing.

The Government has put in place strong measures to drive more sustainable production in the UK:

> promoting energy efficiency through the climate change levy and agreements, and emissions trading

> encouraging waste minimisation and recycling through the landfill tax and the aggregates levy

> integrated pollution prevention and control in many sectors to improve management of waste and emissions to air, land and waste, and

> help and support for business from the Carbon Trust, the Envirowise programme and the Environment Agency.

However, more action is needed if sustainable production is to be mainstreamed in business practice. For example, we need to understand better why business does not always take up opportunities for resource efficiency or to respond to environmental pressures. We need to encourage process re-design, lean manufacturing and ways to use waste from one business as a resource for another, and to integrate sustainable development into all business support programmes. And we need to use regulation and economic instruments intelligently so as to promote cleaner, more competitive businesses.

The Government's approach will be based on the following key areas:

Specific resource efficiency

From April 2005, landfill tax receipts will fund the new Business Resource Efficiency and Waste Programme. Over the next three years, £284 million of funding will be targeted to benefit business through:

> increased support from Envirowise and the Carbon Trust, and for green business and waste minimisation clubs

> the Waste and Resources Action Programme (WRAP), to develop new markets for 'difficult' business wastes, and via the National Industrial Symbiosis Programme to enable waste from one business to become an input for another

> the Department of Trade & Industry's (DTI) technology fund, to support research and development aimed at waste minimisation and management, and energy efficiency

> the Market Transformation Programme, to promote products which result in less waste

> Regional Development Agencies, to co-ordinate local delivery and to carry out strategic resource efficiency projects, and

> the Environment Agency, to tackle fly tipping and ensure a level playing field for business.

Material recycling facilities, UK

Integration with wider business support

Sustainable production is not just an add on, but a fundamental part of business.

> ❯ **The Government will therefore be integrating it more strongly into DTI's overall package of support for business and innovation: for example, through support for research and development and best business practice, and through DTI's innovation and growth research and development teams in key areas such as materials**

Closing the resource loop

Product re-use, re-manufacturing and recycling offer many commercial opportunities, as well as environmental benefits. The Government will favour policies that advance these kinds of market, wherever they make good business and environment sense. For example, additional resources are being made available to initiatives such as WRAP and the National Industrial Symbiosis Programme under the Business Resource Efficiency and Waste programme as part of the wider drive for greater resource efficiency.

Better regulation

The Government has recently launched a programme, with the Environment Agency and other stakeholders, to modernise environmental permitting. We are aiming for more streamlined systems which deliver a better environment and economic efficiencies for both businesses and regulators. The Government will ensure that wherever possible requirements are phased in to fit product life cycles so as to give the greatest scope for innovation to meet new environmental challenges and regulations.

The introduction of NetRegs[17] by the Environment Agency is also designed to help UK business, especially small businesses, to understand environmental regulations. It also provides practical guidance on how to comply with environmental law as well as advice on good practices.

4. Sustainable Consumption

There is huge potential for better products and production processes to deliver improvements without the need for behaviour change from consumers themselves. But there will also be a need for households, businesses and the public sector to consume more efficiently and differently, so that consumption from rising incomes is not accompanied by rising environmental impacts or social injustice. The challenge is big. But so too are the opportunities for innovation to build new markets, products and services.

Much current consumption, and business models based on it, remains unsustainable in the longer term under present technologies and supply patterns. It can be relatively comfortable to talk about sustainable consumption in terms of small behaviours like switching off unnecessary lights or recycling bottles. But our bigger, customary consumption habits pose more difficult issues. For example, the world as a whole could not sustain consumption patterns like those of Western Europe in air and car travel, water use, or diet.

---

[17] See www.netregs.org

We need to understand more about the social and cultural influences which shape our consumption choices, habits and impacts. For example, the rising levels of obesity highlight the complex interaction between social and cultural pressures and how, together with other factors such as income, they determine the food consumption patterns of families and individuals. Part of the challenge is to learn what lies behind these variations. From a public health perspective we need to tackle the overconsumption of 'unhealthy' food at the same time as we tackle the causes of inequalities in relation to food. And we need to address how consumption patterns link to environmental impacts across the whole life cycle of food products.

The Government's current plan of action is based around several important streams of work. These include:

▶ building an evidence base around the environmental impacts arising from households and how patterns of use can be influenced (see also Chapter 2)

▶ working on a new information service – 'Environment Direct' – which will offer public advice on the impacts of different goods and services and how to make the most sustainable consumption choices. It will fill an information gap for both individual consumers and procurement professionals, and expose the whole supply chain to information about the performance of goods and services. We will be consulting on how to take this forward, and if there is broad agreement we hope to have a service up and running in 2006

▶ through a refocused Environmental Action Fund, the Government is supporting voluntary organisations with community level projects which influence behaviour and will deliver sustainable consumption outcomes. We will look to use lessons from these projects to further improve and expand partnership activities of this kind which prove successful in changing consumption patterns. This includes making information available through Community Action 2020 – Together We Can help change consumption patterns on food, transport and other issues

▶ delivering a large-scale deliberative forum to explore public views on sustainable consumption and lifestyles (see Chapter 2), and

▶ the new Round Table on Sustainable Consumption, jointly led by the Sustainable Development Commission and the National Consumer Council, which is developing and building consensus around a practical vision of where and how we might aim to move UK consumption patterns, and of the implications for the traditional business model. The Round Table is due to report in March 2006; following its recommendations the Government will set out a plan for further action on sustainable consumption

Environmental Action Fund (EAF)

Thirty-six projects have been offered Government funding for the three years 2005-2008, totalling £6.75 million, following the latest round of competitive bids for support from the EAF.

These projects cover the whole of England, and involve working with a diverse set of communities on a wide range of issues, which will help deliver sustainable consumption and production outcomes.

Projects being offered support include Envision's Schools and Colleges Programme targeting 16-18 year olds, Global Action Plans' Ecoteam initiative being expanded nationally and the Soil Association's 'Actions Organic' programme.

5. Leading by example in what we do

Consultees highlighted the importance of the Government tackling the issue of sustainable consumption in its procurement of goods, services and buildings and our evidence on "changing behaviours" (Chapter 2) supports this view. The Government accepts this challenge.

Source: 3rd Avenue

Sustainable public procurement

The UK Government buys £13 billion worth of goods and services each year. For the wider public sector this figure is £125 billion. The scale of this purchasing offers an additional policy tool to the traditional approaches such as regulation and economic instruments. Both in the EU and internationally, there is growing pressure on governments to make better use of their purchasing power in this way to deliver their policy goals, for example in areas such as environmental technologies and fair trade.

Efficiency is an essential feature of public sector spending: public money must be well-spent and not wasted. Better purchasing and the delivery of better services are an essential feature of achieving efficiency gains in economic, environmental and social terms. Improving the professionalism of purchasing activity across the public sector and the more widespread use of whole-life costing will go some way to achieving this. But we also need to examine ways to stimulate and enable whole-life accounting – where expenditure looks to achieve the best outcome for the public overall, irrespective of when or where costs and benefits fall.

Sustainable procurement – embedding sustainable development considerations into spending and investment decisions across the public sector – offers many opportunities including:

> avoiding adverse environmental impacts arising on the government estate and in the supply-chain by, for example, reducing waste and emissions

➤ making more efficient use of public resources, for example through reduced energy consumption and reduced packaging

➤ stimulating the market to innovate and to produce more cost effective and sustainable options for all purchasers, and

➤ setting an example for business and the public and demonstrate that government and the wider public sector is serious about sustainable development.

Taking these opportunities offers benefits in environmental, social and economic terms across the public sector, business and wider society. Within the UK, the Government is already using public procurement to deliver policy goals. For example, all central government departments and agencies actively seek to buy timber products from sustainable and legal sources. We have set targets within central civil government for more sustainable procurement in areas such as food, construction and a range of everyday products that meet minimum environmental standards (the so-called "quick-wins"[18]), taking forward the 2003 Report of the Sustainable Procurement Group[19].

➤ **Whilst continuing our efforts to meet these targets across Whitehall, the Government will also examine ways to encourage other organisations to commit to them**

➤ **Our new goal is to be recognised as amongst the leaders in sustainable procurement across EU member states by 2009**

To achieve this goal the Government will:

➤ develop and maintain a robust evidence base on priority areas where sustainable procurement can deliver the most significant environmental and competitiveness outcomes by 2006

➤ develop through consultation further public sector procurement targets in priority areas as revealed by the evidence base; we intend, for example, to put in place a commitment to ensure that new fleet cars purchased by the Government will comply with the existing (and future agreed) European Voluntary Agreements for carbon dioxide emissions

➤ extend the range of mandated products meeting minimum environmental standards (the 'quick wins' list); improve compliance by public sector purchasers and enable suppliers to demonstrate compliance to these standards

➤ embed sustainable development into the existing Office of Government Commerce (OGC) and NHS Purchasing and Supply Agency and work with key markets and work with key public sector suppliers to raise their sustainability understanding and performance, using existing business support programmes where appropriate

➤ work with professional and academic institutions, including the Chartered Institute of Purchasing and Supply, to ensure that sustainable development considerations are embedded in procurement courses and qualifications, and that public sector procurers receive appropriate professional training

---

[18] www.ogcbuyingsolutions.gov.uk/environmental/products/environmental_quickwins.asp
[19] www.sustainable-development.gov.uk/sdig/improving/partf/report03/index.htm

> ❯ develop the 'OGCbuying.solutions' pilot website on sustainable procurement[20] by 2006 into a comprehensive central resource for public sector buyers and suppliers (to sit alongside the proposed public website 'Environment Direct')

> ❯ develop key performance indicators for sustainable procurement activity through working across the public sector, business and other interested parties

> ❯ work closely with the European Commission to measure and assess EU environmental public procurement, in particular related to environmental technologies, with the aim of establishing an EU-wide benchmark target with which to encourage the average performance in 2010 to match that of today's best performing member state

> ❯ work with the Environmental Innovations Advisory Group to demonstrate how public sector purchasers can draw environmental innovations into the market by making a forward commitment through the procurement process, and

> ❯ take action to remove barriers to, and increase the opportunities for, increased sustainable procurement activity.

> ❯ **To ensure we make rapid progress in the most effective way, the Government will appoint in Spring 2005 a business-led Sustainable Procurement Task Force to develop a national action plan for Sustainable Procurement across the public sector by April 2006. The Task Force will build on the work of other bodies active in this field, including the Sustainable Development Commission, the Sustainable Procurement Group and the Strategic Supply-Chain Group.**

6. Catalysing change within the economy and key sectors

The measures above will be applied in all key areas of the economy and will have important implications for business.

It is not possible in this strategy to go into detail about specific products and services in individual sectors; however, we set out below how the Government will work with business on broader, cross-cutting measures, to complement those which have a more direct impact on the products and services that business provide. These are:

> ❯ policies to raise transparency, corporate responsibility and skills in business and other organisations, and

> ❯ how we aim to work with sectors with particularly significant environmental or social impacts. The Round Table on Sustainable Consumption will also have an important contribution to our work with some of these sectors

Finally, we explain how the Government is reviewing its strategy for dealing with waste across the economy as a whole.

---

[20] See www.sustainable-solutions.gov.uk

Sustainable Organisations, Workplaces and Skills

Sustainable organisations – businesses, public bodies, Non-Governmental Organisations (NGOs) or trade unions – can be powerful drivers for more sustainable patterns of consumption and production.

For business, this goes well beyond philanthropy – sustainable businesses are usually more financially profitable. Some 85 per cent of studies on the subject show a positive correlation between environmental governance and/or events, and company financial performance[21]. Managing sustainability performance can improve risk management, identify cost savings, improve reputation and aid communication with shareholders and other stakeholders. Furthermore the challenge of sustainable consumption raises the corporate social responsibility debate to a whole new level, in which businesses must consider the implications, for their business model and product range, of a shift towards more resource-efficient and ethical consumption practices.

Corporate Social Responsibility – The Government's Approach

The Government's vision for corporate social responsibility (CSR) is "to see UK businesses taking account of their economic, social and environmental impacts, and acting to address the key sustainable development challenges based on their core competences wherever they operate – locally, regionally and internationally."

The Government's role is to encourage and enhance CSR at home and abroad. In March 2004, we published for consultation a draft strategic framework on international CSR. In the light of responses, the Government will publish a final version in 2005.

To help support implementation of the Framework, the Government will establish an International CSR Advisory Group to help devise and implement a strategic approach to the critical task of assessing all of the impacts, positive and negative, economic, and social as well as environmental, of the operations of UK businesses across the world, together with an assessment of the effectiveness of the Government's work in encouraging improvement.

We continue to spread best practice, through initiatives such as the UN Global Compact, the OECD Guidelines for Multinational Enterprises, the Voluntary Principles on Security and Human Rights, and through the International Labour Organisation. More details are available at the Government CSR website[22].

Sustainable businesses are typically strongly driven by a set of values or guiding principles, such as those underpinning the UN's Global Compact. They also measure, manage and improve their sustainability performance, and the performance of their supply chains and products in the UK and abroad. Benchmarking metrics and key performance indicators can provide a means to compare organisations.

---

[21] Environment Agency, 2004, 'Corporate Environmental Governance'. Report by Innovest and the Environment Agency.
[22] See www.csr.gov.uk

The Government challenges the FTSE All Share and large private companies to report their performance in a transparent and meaningful way. Some good progress has been made – 145 of the FTSE250 report to some extent on their sustainability performance[23]. To increase these numbers and improve the quality of reporting, the Global Reporting Initiative[24] provides a comprehensive suite of performance indicators, and we have produced a practical set of Environmental Reporting Guidelines[25].

Operating and Financial Review

From April 2005, the Government is introducing an enabling framework – the Operating and Financial Review (OFR) – so that listed companies consider sustainable development issues alongside financial information. Wherever companies face environmental risks and uncertainties, or social, community and employee issues, we expect their OFRs to report on policies and performance to the extent necessary for shareholders to assess the company's strategies and their potential to succeed.

So, for example, Directors will need to consider how their company is gearing up to operate in a carbon-constrained world, where UK carbon dioxide emissions will need to fall by at least 60 per cent over the next fifty years. In parallel, the Accounts Modernisation Directive will introduce requirements for large private companies to report on environmental or employee matters to the extent necessary for an understanding of the company's development, performance or position.

The Government is seeking to enable investors to engage more effectively in driving business change. As well as the OFR, we are working with big institutional investors, lenders and insurers. The London Principles Project[26], a compendium of best practice including a proposed set of seven principles by which financial market mechanisms can best promote the financing of sustainable development, is an example of the City of London's leadership in this area.

The amendment to the Pensions Act 1995 requiring pension schemes to state the extent to which they consider social, environmental or ethical issues in their investment strategy will continue to raise the profile of socially responsible investment. And within the Charity Sector the new Statement of Recommended Practice highlights the need for charities to communicate with their stakeholders and the public how ethical considerations, which include sustainability considerations, influence their investment decisions.

The Government will also look at what can be done to empower individuals to make sustainable choices in how their money is invested. This could be helped by organisations offering employees a choice of an environmental or ethical fund for additional pension contributions.

For organisations generally, the institutional, accountability and other mechanisms will vary, but the values enshrined in corporate responsibility and citizenship are just as relevant. The Government wants to see greater uptake of robust and accredited environmental management systems (EMSs), such as EMAS, ISO 14001 and BS8555. Equally important is to enhance the standard of certification and improve the quality of EMSs so that they lead more predictably to performance improvements. Part of this is

---

[23] Salterbaxter/Context, 2004 'Directions: trends in CSR reporting 2003–2004'. Joint report by salterbaxter and Context.
[24] See www.globalreporting.org/
[25] See www.defra.gov.uk/environment/envrp/index.htm
[26] See www.cityoflondon.gov.uk/Corporation/living_environment/sustainability/sustainable_finance.htm#lp

ensuring that independent and accredited verification procedures are robust and applied in a consistent way.

The Government supported the SIGMA (Sustainability – Integrated Guidelines for Management) project[27] and its aims of providing clear advice and tools to help organisations manage and improve their contribution to sustainable development and improve environmental performance. The SIGMA Guidelines launched in September 2003 are also a key element in current projects being led by BSI[28] in the UK and ISO internationally[29] to examine a possible standard providing guidelines on social responsibility.

Several reports[30] have identified an economy-wide gap in skills needed to deliver more sustainable consumption and production. This is being tackled through the Department for Education and Skills' Sustainable Development Action Plan described in Chapter 2. The Government has established a CSR Academy to support development of skills for corporate responsibility, and is working with professional bodies to integrate sustainable development competencies into their standards.

Many lasting changes in the workplace are delivered in partnership by employers, managers and workers[31]. Trade Union Congress (TUC) surveys[32] of union members have shown support for unions promoting good environmental practice.

> **To galvanise action, the Government is working with the TUC and the Trade Union Sustainable Development Advisory Committee (TUSDAC) to develop a Trade Union Sustainability Strategy**

Business Sectors

The Government will also work more generally to build on work since 1999 with the **Pioneers Group** of trade associations and sector bodies to help them develop their own sector sustainability strategies. Eighteen sectors have now published at least initial strategies and there are several more in preparation.

The Government believes that this is a good basis on which to build but we now aim to intensify our work with business to increase our joint understanding of how to deliver long term decoupling in key sectors and to put in place measures to support that transition. This will involve examining the broader range of options available in specific sectors for achieving environmental outcomes and increased productivity from doing things differently, including:

> enhanced skills through formal training and/or awareness raising

> workplace initiatives inspired and led by the workforce

> business support programmes and grant schemes for eco-design, resource efficiency, innovation, and/or supply-chain management

---

[27] See www.projectsigma.com/default.asp
[28] See www.bsi-global.com/British_Standards/sustainability/index.xalter
[29] See www.iso.org/iso/en/info/Conferences/SRConference/nwip.htm
[30] PIU report, Energy White Paper and Changing Patterns.
[31] See www.sustainableworkplace.co.uk for further information
[32] See www.tuc.org.uk/sustainableworkplace/Prospect_Environ_lft.pdf

> benchmarking, reporting and indicators

> identifying opportunities for better regulation

> sector specific fiscal instruments, voluntary agreements or trading schemes

> procurement policies, and

> product standards and/or labelling schemes.

Strategies should provide sectors with a framework to identify threats to the sector from unsustainable practices, and opportunities to benefit from more sustainable ways of working.

> **The Government will launch a new Sector Sustainability Challenge by summer 2005**

This will support selected collaborative projects focused on taking forward sectoral or supply chain initiatives to put Sustainable Consumption and Production into practical action.

The sectors outlined below are among those which have a particularly strong influence on the sustainability of goods and services consumed in the UK.

Retailers

Retailers both shape the sustainability of their supply chains and determine the range of products and services available to consumers. Retailers also have a role to play in cutting down on energy, water use and waste in their own operations. The British Retail Consortium has already developed a sector strategy to identify impacts, set targets and monitor progress. Some retailers have also taken steps such as offering sustainably sourced products such as timber or fish, promoting fair traded goods, reducing hazardous substances in products, minimising packaging or participating in awareness raising campaigns.

The Prime Minister has said that, in future, consumers should expect that environmental responsibility is as fundamental to the products they buy as health and safety is now[33]. Environment Direct should help to highlight good and bad practice. We will also continue to work with retailers through, for example:

> WRAP and Defra working with retailers and local authorities to pilot new ways to encourage householders to recycle their waste at supermarkets

> working with retailers on environmental impact assessments of their products

> help from Envirowise for retailers to work in partnerships with key suppliers to improve business efficiency and reduce waste, and

> working with retailers and suppliers to prepare for the new European chemicals strategy.

---

[33] Prime Minister's Speech on Climate Change, 14 September 2004.

Tourism

Tourism is one of the world's largest industries, accounting for nearly an eighth of global Gross Domestic Product. It is one of the more complex, cross-cutting areas of economic activity, with huge social and environmental interactions, that needs to be approached from the perspective of sustainable consumption and production. For example, it has massive potential to support the economic and social development of poorer countries. At the same time, there is a need to minimise the potential which tourism also has for damaging the environment and indigenous cultures.

Ramblers on hillside looking over valley
Source: 3rd Avenue

The Government aims to build greater cooperation with the UK's outbound tourism industry and with international partners to promote more sustainable patterns of tourism globally. As a first step we have helped to set up the Travel Foundation, which is developing mechanisms through which tourism can make a positive contribution to local people and the environment.

We also recognise that a more coordinated and strategic approach is needed across government and industry. The Government is setting up new arrangements across departments so that the many dimensions of sustainable tourism can be better addressed, both for tourism within the UK and for UK tourism overseas.

Within the UK we seek a tourism sector which grows and thrives by actively embracing sustainable development principles. Regional Development Agencies develop and implement Regional Sustainable Tourism Strategies with the aim of mainstreaming tourism into their wider actions to achieve sustainable economic growth, through their Regional Economic Strategies. We will support their actions with the help of local authority Beacon Councils and private sector initiatives like the Green Tourism Business Scheme.

Construction and construction minerals

The construction sector makes an important contribution not only in the use and management of resources, including minerals and wood, but also in shaping how we use them in our everyday life.

The **Code for Sustainable Buildings** (see Chapter 4) will establish new voluntary standards for resource efficiency. In addition, the Government will continue to demonstrate what can be achieved by good design and management through our Millennium Communities programme. Through our work with the Housing Forum, English Partnerships, and others, the Government will continue to actively promote the use of good quality Modern Methods of Construction which can offer resource efficiency through reducing waste, better levels of productivity, energy efficiency, and improved health and safety.

It is also important to encourage individual sectors to develop plans to work towards delivering sustainable development. Individual sector sustainability strategies have already been developed in civil engineering, brick, steel, cement and concrete. The Aggregates Levy encourages economy in the use of construction aggregates and more recycling of construction and demolition waste in place of new quarrying. Planning policy aims to minimise the impacts of necessary quarrying on the landscape.

Transport

The design and use of transport is an important element of encouraging more Sustainable Consumption and Production. Chapter 4 outlines many actions on transport that will equally contribute to Sustainable Consumption and Production. For example, the Powering Future Vehicles Strategy[34] work on clean, low-carbon vehicles and fuels, and the activities of the Low Carbon Vehicle Partnership[35]. The development of our thinking on sustainable consumption, described earlier in this chapter, will also help us to understand what we can do to influence transport choices in the context of encouraging more sustainable lifestyles and business practices.

Smarter choices – Changing the way we travel

The Department for Transport published a guide 'Making Smarter Choices Work' in December 2004 to help and encourage local authorities to recognise the potential benefits of "soft" transport measures and make them an integral part of their transport strategies, so reducing congestion and giving people genuine travel choices.

The research on which the document was based 'Smarter Choices – Changing the way we travel' was published in July 2004 and showed the benefits to be gained from a range of measures such as workplace and school travel plans, personalised travel planning, public transport information and marketing, travel awareness campaigns, car clubs and car sharing, teleworking, teleconferencing and home shopping.[36]

The Government has already put in place two key initiatives to take forward smarter choices:

▶ £50 million for 2004/5 and 2005/6 to help schools develop and implement travel plans, and

▶ £10 million over 5 years to transform Darlington, Peterborough and Worcester into sustainable travel demonstration towns.

The Government will also continue to promote the development of Freight Quality Partnerships (FQPs) by local authorities. FQPs are a template for industry and local government working together to develop more efficient, safer and cleaner means of local goods distribution. Over 40 FQPs have been established in England so far.

We will also work with the haulage industry to adopt more fuel-efficient practices. For example, the Government has announced a further year of funding (£3 million) for some of the most successful programmes under the Road Haulage Modernisation Fund.

---

[34] See www.dft.gov.uk/stellent/groups/dft_roads/documents/page/dft_roads_506885.hcsp
[35] See www.lowcvp.org.uk
[36] DfT, 2004, 'Smarter Choices' at www.dft.gov.uk

Food

Achieving more sustainable consumption and production of food is a major challenge. The production of food includes agricultural production, manufacturing, transportation of crops and products, storage, retailing and food services. Food consumption by the householder involves shopping trips, refrigeration/freezing, cooking and waste disposal.

When all environmental impacts are taken into account across the life cycle of goods and services, whether in the UK or abroad, food may be one of the most environmentally significant aspects of consumption. For example, consumption of food in the UK is responsible for global greenhouse gas emissions equivalent to 22 per cent of the UK's overall total.

Our strategy for sustainable food and farming[37] sets out how industry, Government and consumers can work together to secure a sustainable future for our farming and food industries, as viable industries contributing to a better environment and healthy and prosperous communities.

In parallel, the Government is working with industry on a sustainability strategy for economic, environmental and social improvements in the wider food industry. This will be the basis for longer term objectives for sustainability in the food industry.

Environmental Industries

Innovative environmental technologies can bring new business opportunities, open up developing markets and enhance competitiveness, at the same time as helping to meet environmental objectives. Their potential to contribute to a sustainable economy and be a driver for new business and jobs is increasingly being recognised around the world.

In 2002, the global market for environmental goods and services was estimated at $515 billion – comparable to the international aerospace or pharmaceutical markets – and forecast to be worth $688 billion by 2010. We want the UK to be a leading player in this significant and rapidly growing market.

The UK environmental industry is a dynamic and growing sector which makes an important – and increasing – contribution to the economy. Data gathered in 2004 showed that companies identifying themselves as working in the environmental technology sector now have a turnover of around £25 billion, and account for around 400 000 jobs.

But the sector is facing increasingly stiff competition from suppliers both at home and abroad. To sustain its growth in the coming decade, the UK must improve its ability to turn new ideas and emerging technologies into more innovative, high value products, processes and services. We have launched a refocused joint DTI/Defra Environmental Industries Unit and tasked it with promoting the needs of the sector by encouraging innovation.

➤ **The Government will implement a package of measures to tackle barriers to the commercialisation of environmental innovations identified by the business-led Environmental Innovations Advisory Group by March 2006**

---

[37] Defra, 2002, 'Strategy for Sustainable Farming and Food: Facing the Future' at www.defra.gov.uk/farm/sustain/default.htm

7. Sustainable Waste Management

The overall objective of government policy on waste is to protect human health and the environment by producing less waste and by using it as a resource wherever possible. Through more sustainable waste management – reduction, re-use, recycling, composting and using waste as a source of energy – the Government aims to break the link between economic growth and the environmental impact of waste. Business, consumers, voluntary organisations and local authorities all have a role to play.

The 'Waste Strategy 2000'[38] included a commitment for a "root-and-branch" review in 2010, with smaller reviews in 2005 and 2015.

> **The Government intends to present the conclusions of the first review by the end of 2005.**

This review provides an opportunity to assess current policies and delivery mechanisms and to evaluate progress on outcomes. Through the review, the Government will be able to reassess assumptions that have been made about costs, growth in waste and potentially achievable recovery and recycling rates based on new data, advances in technology and a better understanding of environmental, economic and social impacts of dealing with waste.

We have already made progress on a number of fronts, but there is much more we can all do to prevent waste occurring at source and to make the maximum use of it as a resource. The Waste and Resources Action Programme will continue its work with retailers on waste minimisation and will take forward its initiatives on stimulating the market for recyclates.

> **The Government will engage with stakeholders in Spring 2005 on revised guidance on the definition of waste.**

A key objective of the revised guidance will be to help industry and regulators better to determine when waste has been fully recovered so that it ceases to be "waste" and is transformed into a resource.

[38] Defra, 2000, 'Waste Strategy 2000' at www.defra.gov.uk/environment/waste/strategy/cm4693/index.htm

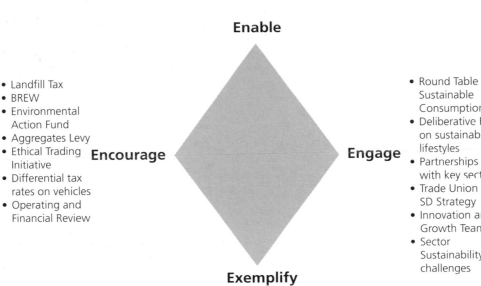

Our integrated approach for sustainable consumption and production

- Environment Direct
- Envirowise and market transformation programmes
- CSR Academy
- Sustainable Design Forum
- DTI's Technology Fund
- Support for social enterprises

Enable

- Landfill Tax
- BREW
- Environmental Action Fund
- Aggregates Levy
- Ethical Trading Initiative
- Differential tax rates on vehicles
- Operating and Financial Review

Encourage

Engage

- Round Table on Sustainable Consumption
- Deliberative Forum on sustainable lifestyles
- Partnerships with key sectors
- Trade Union SD Strategy
- Innovation and Growth Teams
- Sector Sustainability challenges

Exemplify

- Goal to be one of the EU leaders in sustainable procurement by 2009
- Draft national action plan for Sustainable Procurement across the public sector

8. Evidence and indicators

Policies on sustainable consumption and production require a variety of evidence – for example, on the life cycle impacts of goods and services, on the links between environment and competitiveness, on individual values and behaviour, on the impacts of UK and EU consumption on other countries, and on the impacts of policy measures. Compared with some more specific areas, such as climate change, understanding of these issues is at an earlier stage. A key element of our strategy will therefore be to improve our evidence base, in partnership with others including the research community, business, consumer bodies and environmental organisations. This will include pulling together the range of existing research, including the work of the expert group to be established alongside our international CSR framework, as well as learning from on the ground, local projects.

> **The Government will be discussing and developing our plans with these stakeholders, beginning in spring 2005**

Key indicators of sustainable consumption and production include those which show the extent of 'decoupling' – how successful we are in breaking the link between economic growth and environmental damage. A number of the UK Government Strategy Indicators take the form of 'decoupling indicators' selected from a revised set of sustainable consumption and production decoupling indicators on which we consulted last year. The full set of revised 'decoupling indicators', to be published separately, will provide more detailed reporting than can be accommodated by the indicators selected here to support the UK Government Strategy.

The indicators listed below include all indicators within the UK Framework set that are relevant to sustainable consumption and production and in addition 'decoupling' and other indicators relevant to the priorities of the UK Government Strategy.

Measuring our Progress – Decoupling impacts

> **Greenhouse gas emissions[*2]:** Kyoto target and CO_2 emissions
> **CO_2 emissions by end user:** industry, domestic, transport (excluding international aviation), other
> **Aviation and shipping emissions[1]:** greenhouse gases from UK-based international aviation and shipping fuel bunkers, and GDP
> **Household energy use[2]:** domestic CO_2 emissions and household final consumption expenditure
> **Road transport:** CO_2, NO_x, PM_{10} emissions and GDP
> **Private vehicles[1]:** CO_2 emissions and car-km and household final consumption expenditure
> **Road freight:** CO_2 emissions and tonne-km, tonnes and GDP
> **Manufacturing sector[1]:** CO_2, NO_x, SO_2, PM_{10} emissions and GVA
> **Agriculture sector[1]:** fertiliser input, farmland bird population, and ammonia and methane emissions and output
> **Service sector[1]:** CO_2, NO_x emissions and GVA
> **Public sector[1]:** CO_2, NO_x emissions and GVA
> **Emissions of air pollutants[1]:** SO_2, NO_x, NH_3 and PM_{10} emissions and GDP
> **River quality[*2]:** rivers of good (a) biological (b) chemical quality

Resource use

➤ **Resource use*[1]:** Domestic Material Consumption and GDP
➤ **Fish stocks*[1]:** fish stocks around the UK within sustainable limits
➤ **Water resource use[1]:** total abstractions from non-tidal surface and ground water sources and GDP
➤ **Domestic water consumption[2]:** domestic water consumption per head
➤ **Land recycling[2]:** (a) new dwellings built on previously developed land or through conversions (b) all new development on previously developed land

Waste

➤ **Waste*[1]:** arisings by (a) sector (b) method of disposal
➤ **Household waste[2]:** (a) arisings (b) recycled or composted

Other contextual indicators

➤ **Economic output*:** Gross Domestic Product
➤ **Productivity:** UK output per worker
➤ **Investment:** (a) total investment (b) social investment relative to GDP
➤ **Demography:** population and population of working age (contextual indicator)
➤ **Households and dwellings:** households, single person households, and dwelling stock (contextual indicator)

Note some indicators are relevant to other parts of the Strategy and are also listed in other chapters.

* Indicator is included in the UK Framework Indicators

[1] Indicator is within the revised set of Sustainable Consumption and Production 'decoupling indicators'

[2] Indicator is similar but not the same as an indicator within the revised set of Sustainable Consumption and Production Indicators

Role of Business in Sustainable Development

Business has a key role in sustainable development – by taking account of their economic, social and environmental impacts, tackling the key sustainable development challenges, and generating wealth and jobs. This runs through all four priorities and is highlighted in each of the chapters.

Business investment, enterprise and trading are essential in creating the wealth to tackle poverty and other social challenges at home and abroad. Government has an important role to play through active economic, social and environmental policies that support or stimulate action. But ultimately it is the action taken by businesses themselves that will deliver a supply of products and services that are clean, resource-efficient, and fair to employees and communities. These include:

> more systematic management of the impacts of their products and processes, of their transport and distribution operations, and of their supply chains

> building stakeholder confidence by being more open and transparent through reporting against meaningful key performance indicators and targets

> actively keeping customers informed through product declarations or labelling, and

> by communicating sustainability aims to the workforce and local community.

Organisations, individuals and the environment can also benefit from developing the potential opportunities for new business models. Service innovation, for example, can offer potential efficiency gains. Traditionally, business profits are tied to increased product sales. If suppliers instead supply a service, rather than a product, alternative opportunities for profit and reductions in resource use are created. A company could shift from selling barrels of chemicals, to selling the service the chemical is used for, such as cleaning or degreasing. An energy supplier could shift from selling energy to providing a warm home service. The approach is based on aligning the incentives of customer and supplier. Both can gain from cost reductions derived from improved resource efficiency.

British Gas – *'here to HELP'*

BITC Awards for Excellence 2004 – Big Tick winner.

'here to HELP' is the first national integrated fuel and household poverty programme, involving private, public and voluntary sector partners, to be developed by an energy supplier.

The 'here to HELP' programme, initiated by British Gas in July 2002, brings together local authorities, housing associations and seven major national charities in delivering a 'One Stop' shop solution. The programme, which aims to reach half a million households, provides a comprehensive range of help for poorer households. The £150 million, 3 year programme is on course to deliver 40 per cent of British Gas's fuel poverty energy saving target for 2002-2005. The integrated funding approach and economies of scale from working in concentrated areas is enabling the target to be reached at significantly less cost than traditional programmes.

To date, 295 000 homes have been identified, and 80 000 households had been surveyed. This has resulted in benefits assessments identifying £3.6 million in unclaimed benefits; which is a potential average increase of £1 400 per qualifying household a year. And public perception of British Gas as a socially responsible company increased from 53 per cent (in March 2003) to 71 per cent (by November 2003). – source: TNS SR Tracker.

Within the UK, businesses of all types face growing economic competition to develop new ideas, raise their productivity, and create new products and high-value services. And the intangible asset of corporate reputation is now a vital part of building and keeping market value, and is increasingly vulnerable to perceived failures in social and environmental responsibility. A business's bottom line is of course important – its fundamental goal must be to make a profit. But as the case studies of Business in The Community[36] award winners show such actions can have significant benefits in terms of enhanced corporate reputation, improved staff recruitment and retention rates, reduced costs and can offer a sustainable competitive advantage to differentiate businesses from others in the marketplace.

Kent Art Printers Ltd (KAP)

BITC Awards for Excellence 2004 – Big Tick winner.

Kent Art Printers (KAP) is a family-owned printing company based in Chatham, Kent with 35 employees. Over the past 15 years it has:

> introduced alcohol-free printing, vegetable-based inks, and internet-based proofing

> extended recycling/reuse of waste, and sourced electricity from renewables

> promoted a healthy work balance with a single working shift and low overtime dependence

> organised regular school visits to the site as part of the science curriculum

> provided work placements opportunities for local schools, and a French Lycée in Poitiers

> sponsored awards schemes – such as those at the local art college, and

> supported local charities by donating staff time, printing & other resources.

KAP has benefited from its socially and environmentally responsible actions, through creating a 'niche' for itself as a green and socially responsible printer, who people want to work for and customers want to work with, and as an organisation that delivers a positive impact on the local community that is disproportionate to its relatively modest size.

Key actions and what Government will do to make them happen include:

> **Sustainable design – enabling consumers make more sustainable choices by "designing it in". We will set up a Sustainable Design Forum to mainstream sustainability into product design**

> **Expansion of the Market Transformation Programme into wider life-cycle issues of key products**

> **Giving stakeholders information about impacts – Environment Direct will give consumers information about products, and the Operating and Financial Review will mean business social, environment and community impacts are reported alongside financial information where necessary**

---

[36] Further information is available at www.bitc.org.uk on a unique movement of 700 companies aiming to inspire and support business in continually improving its positive impact on society

> **Innovation to meet sustainability challenges and new regulatory requirements** – we will integrate sustainability into our business support, and phase in regulation to fit product cycles

> **"Selling sustainability"** – we will launch a new sector sustainability challenge to trade associations and leading firms

> **Sustainable investment** – we will engage financial institutions to help drive business change

> **Sustainable workplaces** – the DfES Sustainable Development Action Plan, the Trade Union Sustainability Strategy and work with Sector Skills Councils will raise awareness, engagement and skills in the workplace

> **Reducing greenhouse gas emissions.** We will support this through measures including promoting energy efficiency and renewables

> **Community impacts** – engaging business in community strategies through initiatives such as the Business Brokers scheme and Corporate Challenge

> **Contributing to regional sustainable development** – guidance to RDAs on preparing Regional Economic Strategies will cover sustainable development

> **International impacts** – maximise the positive contribution that business can make to international sustainable development. We will set up an Advisory Group on measuring the impacts of UK companies and drive for a successful outcome on the trade and environment and trade and development elements of the Doha Development Agenda, and the inclusion of sustainable development in EU bilateral trade agreements

Strategic Supply Chain Group (SSSG)

Driving sustainable production and consumption through strategic procurement and supply chain management

The Strategic Supply Chain Group brings together Senior Executives and Board level representatives, from a wide range of organizations, to consider environmental and sustainability issues in supply chains. It works to spread best practice through the supply networks of its members and is building links with organisations nationally and internationally.

Actions and outputs of the group include:

> a business case for Sustainable Supply Chain Management – for Chief Executives

> a risk management approach to sustainable supply chain management – guidance document for practitioners

> Sustainable Procurement Training – a series of one-day workshops for businesses and public sector organisations

> case studies of good practice in sustainable, cost-effective supply management Identifying key sustainable development issues in the global supply chains of members, and

> developing tools and techniques to manage significant issues, including: CO_2 strategies, fleet management, waste reduction through procurement, sustainable construction, innovative sustainable product design and benchmarking sustainable procurement.

Social Enterprises

Social Enterprises are businesses with primarily social objectives whose surpluses are principally reinvested for that purpose in the business or in the community, rather than being driven by the need to maximise profit for shareholders and owners. Successful social enterprises can play an important role in helping deliver on many of the Government's key policy objectives by:

> helping to drive up productivity and competitiveness

> contributing to socially inclusive wealth creation

> enabling individuals and communities to work towards regenerating their local neighbourhoods

> showing new ways to deliver public services, and

> helping to develop an inclusive society and active citizenship.

The Government's vision is of dynamic and sustainable social enterprise strengthening an inclusive and growing economy. They are already making a valuable contribution through local food initiatives, community transport schemes, fair trade products and recycling schemes.

Bulky Bob's is a real life example of 'joined up' service delivery. It shows how a local authority can achieve best value, improve services, tackle poverty and support the growth and sustainability of social enterprise. Launched in 2000, Bulky Bob's, a wholly owned subsidiary of the FRC Group charity, won a contract with Liverpool City Council to collect bulky domestic waste. The enterprise calls at more than 60,000 homes every year and aims to re-use, recycle and refurbish at least 30 per cent by tonnage of the items collected. The enterprise is committed to creating employment and providing training and has an 89 per cent success rate of getting people from long term unemployment into jobs.

Mike Storey – leader of Liverpool City Council
"With Bulky Bob's we are showing how a new social business can genuinely join things up. Residents get a much improved and reliable collection service. Families in need get decent cheap furniture. Unemployed people get jobs in collecting, sorting, re-cycling and selling. Everyone wins."

Chapter 4
Confronting the Greatest Threat: Climate Change and Energy

The facts

> Projections of future climate change indicate that global average temperature could rise by between 1.4°C and 5.8°C between 1990 and 2100 depending on emissions[1]

> By the 2080s the annual number of people at risk from coastal flooding due to surges could increase from about 10 million to as many as 80 million worldwide, with around half of the increase in the poorest parts of Asia[2]

> After adjusting for natural land movements, the average sea level around the UK is now about 10cm higher than it was in 1900[3]

> Forecasts have suggested that by 2030 emissions from aviation could amount to about a quarter of the UK's total contribution to climate change[4]

> Every household in the UK creates around six tonnes of carbon dioxide every year – enough to fill six hot air balloons 10 metres in diameter. By taking energy efficiency measures, the average household could reduce this by one-third (2 tonnes) and save £200 per year[5]

[1] Intergovernmental Panel on Climate Change (IPCC), 2001, Third Assessment Report at www.ipcc.ch
[2] Defra funded Fast-Track Research Nicholls R. J., 2004, 'Coastal flooding and wetland loss in the 21st century Global Environmental Change', Volume 14, pages 69–86.
[3] UK Climate Impacts Programme at www.ukcip.org.uk/climate_change/how_uk_change.asp
[4] DfT, 2003, 'The Future of Air Transport'. In this context, UK aviation is defined as all domestic services, plus all international departures from the UK. There is as yet no international agreement on the allocation of international aviation emissions to individual states.
[5] The Energy Saving Trust, 2004, at www.est.org.uk/myhome/climatechange/stats/homeenvironment/

Summary

The effects of a changing climate can already be seen. Temperatures and sea levels are rising, ice and snow cover are declining. The consequences could be catastrophic for the natural world and society. The scientific consensus is that most of the warming observed over the last fifty years is attributable to human activity, through emissions of greenhouse gases – such as carbon dioxide and methane – into the atmosphere. We need to make a profound change in our use of energy and other activities that release these gases. And we need to prepare for the changes in climate that are now already unavoidable.

Taking it on consultation responses

Responses to the 'Taking it on – developing UK sustainable development strategy together' consultation questions on climate change and energy, fell broadly into three categories proposing (i) more use of taxes and other fiscal measures, (ii) more education and awareness raising activities and (iii) Government leading by example. Two specific policy areas were singled out: land use planning – which was identified as a key lever for desired change, and aviation as a sector needing better regulation to control its contribution to total greenhouse gas emissions.

1. Our approach

Sustainable development and climate change are two vitally important and interrelated challenges facing us in the 21st century. Our ability to develop more sustainably will determine the speed and degree of climate change we experience. And as the climate changes the choices available to us to develop sustainably will change.

We need to significantly reduce our greenhouse gas emissions – at home, at work and when travelling, so that we can change the course of climate change. Furthermore, some climate change is now inevitable due to our past greenhouse gas emissions. We need to adapt – at the same time as we act to reduce emissions – to better manage the future impacts of climate change on the environment, economy and society.

"Climate Change is the most severe problem we are facing today"

**Sir David King,
UK Government's chief
scientific adviser, 2004**

*Flooding in Chertsey, Surrey
Source: 3rd Avenue*

What will climate change mean for the world in the 21st century?

Higher temperatures would cause the ocean volume to expand, and melting glaciers and ice caps would add more water. If the higher end of our forecasted rise in sea-levels is reached, heavily populated coastlines of such countries as Bangladesh would be flooded, some nations may disappear entirely (such as the island state of the Maldives), freshwater supplies for billions of people could be fouled, and the impact could spur mass migrations.

Agricultural yields are expected to drop in most tropical and sub-tropical regions for every degree rise in ambient temperature. Drying of continental interiors, such as central Asia, the African Sahel, and the Great Plains of the United States, is also forecast. These changes could cause, at a minimum, disruptions in land use and food supply. And the range of diseases such as malaria may expand and spread.

United Nations Framework Convention on Climate Change, www.unfccc.int

What will climate change mean for the UK in the 21st century?

Relative sea level will continue to rise around most of the UK's shoreline. By the 2080s sea levels in the Thames Estuary may have risen by as much as 86 cm.[a]

Winters will become wetter and summers may become drier everywhere. By the 2050s average soil moisture in the summer may be reduced by up to 30 per cent over large parts of England. By the 2080s this could be a loss of 40 per cent or more.[a]

High summer temperatures will become more frequent and very cold winters will become increasingly rare.[a] A very hot summer, such as that experienced across Europe in 2003, may occur as often as one year in two in the 2040s, and could be considered a 'cold' summer by the end of the century.[b]

Increased numbers of heat related deaths, cases of food poisoning and skin cancer and a higher risk of major disasters caused by severe winter gales and flooding. By 2050s, heat-related deaths may increase by 2,000 cases per year, cases of food poisoning by perhaps 10,000 per year and skin cancer may increase by 5,000 cases per year. However, cold-related winter deaths may reduce by perhaps 20,000 per year.[c]

a: Figures from: 'Climate Change Scenarios for the United Kingdom: the UKCIP02 Briefing Report', 2002, Tyndall Centre for Climate Change Research, University of East Anglia. Current values based on a 1961-1990 average, predicted values based on the High emissions scenario. Available from http://www.ukcip.org.uk

b: Stott, P. A., Stone D. A., and Allen M. R., 2004, 'Human Contribution to the European heatwave of 2003', Nature, volume 432, pages 610–614.

c: Figures from: 'Health effects of Climate Change,' 2001, produced for the Department of Health. Predicted case numbers based on the Medium-High emissions scenario.

2. Emission targets and progress to date

In 2003, the UK Government committed to the long-term goal to reduce carbon dioxide emissions by some 60 per cent by about 2050 with real progress by 2020. We were one of the first countries to announce such an ambitious and far-reaching goal.

This goal was in addition to two existing UK targets:

▶ the Kyoto Protocol target to reduce UK greenhouse gas emissions by 12.5 per cent below base year levels over the period 2008-12[6], and

▶ the national goal to reduce carbon dioxide emissions by 20 per cent below 1990 levels by 2010

[6] Under the Kyoto Protocol, cuts in the three major gases – carbon dioxide, methane and nitrous oxide are measured against a base year of 1990. Cuts in hydrofluorocarbons, perfluorocarbons and sulphur hexafluoride are measured against a baseline of 1995.

Why do we have targets for greenhouse gas and carbon dioxide emissions?

Our target under the Kyoto Protocol relates to the reduction in emissions of the six main greenhouse gases – carbon dioxide (CO_2), methane (CH_4), nitrous oxide (NO_2), hydrofluorocarbons (HFCs), perfluorocarbons (PFCs) and sulphur hexafluoride (SF_6).

The UK Government also decided to set national goals for just one of these gases – carbon dioxide. This is because carbon dioxide is by far the most important of the six gases, and will be responsible for about two thirds of the expected future climate change. It is also one of the more difficult gases to control.

Latest projections show that the UK is well on course to meet its Kyoto target, which is a significant achievement. However, more needs to be done to achieve our national 2010 goal. Current estimated projections, taking into account measures within the UK Climate Change Programme (CCP) show that carbon dioxide emissions are expected to be about 14 per cent below 1990 levels by 2010 rather than 20 per cent. Through the current review of the UK Climate Change Programme the Government is committed to evaluating the existing programme measures and aims to publish a revised programme in summer 2005. We are working closely together within Government to ensure that we consider all aspects of the costs and benefits of reducing emissions across all sectors, and to ensure that we can remain on track towards our targets and long-term goals.

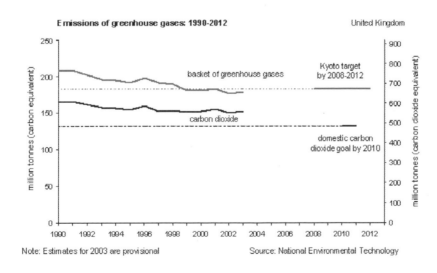

Emissions of carbon dioxide and the Kyoto Protocol's basket of greenhouse gases between 1990 and 2003.

3. International framework

The UK can, and should, show leadership in tackling climate change, but as we are responsible for only 2.2 per cent of global emissions we need others to act with us.

> ❯ **The UK Government will continue to work with other countries to establish both a consensus on the need for change and firm commitments to reduce carbon emissions, using the UN Framework Convention on Climate Change (UNFCCC)**

This will have benefits for both long-term global economic development and human welfare, and insure against the potential reduction in UK competitiveness from isolated climate change action.

UN Framework Convention on Climate Change and the Kyoto Protocol

The Kyoto Protocol came into effect on the 16 February 2005. It provides the first ever framework for international action with binding targets and timetables for reducing greenhouse gas emissions. Over 140 countries have ratified it. The Protocol represents a very important milestone in tackling climate change.

But the Kyoto Protocol is only a first step, mapping action only for the first commitment period (until 2012). The world's largest emitter – the US – and a number of other countries have made it clear that they will not participate in the Kyoto Protocol, and it is vitally important that we enter into discussion with all parties on action beyond 2012.

Kyoto Protocol

In December 1997, over 160 nations met in Kyoto, Japan to discuss the United Nations Framework Convention on Climate Change (UNFCCC). The outcome of the meeting was the Kyoto Protocol, in which developed nations set targets for limiting their greenhouse gas emissions. Countries that ratified the Protocol could engage in emissions trading with each other, which would reward countries achieving reductions in excess of their targets.

In 2005, the UK holds the presidencies of the G8 and EU, and the Prime Minister has placed climate change at the top of the agenda in both arenas, providing us with an invaluable opportunity to raise the profile of this issue worldwide and to complement and reinforce the UNFCCC process.

G8 and EU Presidencies

The Prime Minister, in his 2004 speech to the Prince of Wales Business and Environment Programme, stated three broad aims for the UK's **G8** presidency to tackle climate change:

> to build a solid foundation on the science so as to be in a position to reach global agreement on the urgency of the problem. There has been much new scientific information on climate change since the IPCC's 3rd Assessment Report came out in 2001

> to reach agreement on a process to speed up the science, technology and other measures necessary to meet the threat, and

> to engage countries outside the G8 who have growing energy needs, like China and India, on how these needs can be met sustainably and how they can adapt to the impacts which are already inevitable.

The UK will use its Presidency of the **European Union** in the second half of 2005 to continue the development of an EU medium-term and long-term strategy for tackling climate change. This will support discussions at the 11th Conference of the Parties to the UN Framework Convention in 2005 on further international action to combat climate change. Another key priority will be raising the profile of the growing problem of aviation emissions.

Financial assistance and technology transfer

International co-operation plays a crucial role in tackling climate change. The UK will continue to work with developing countries in tackling climate change, and to facilitate the transfer of technology and improve access to relevant financial assistance. The Government will look at ways to ensure that UK financial assistance to developing countries maximises opportunities for adopting low and zero carbon technologies and will encourage international organisations such as the World Bank to do the same.

In many countries, especially in Africa and South Asia, most people still have no access to electricity or modern fuels for cooking, heating and productive enterprises[7]. This is a serious constraint to those countries' economic growth and to their efforts to reduce poverty and the effects of poverty. As part of our assistance to less developed countries, the UK is working with international partners to improve access to modern forms of energy.

While increased access to modern energy will increase carbon emissions from developing countries, this will displace inefficient and wasteful forms of energy use, such as wood burning on primitive stoves and the use of candles and kerosene for lighting. There will be major health and other social benefits as well as greater employment and income opportunities. Efforts to reduce global carbon emissions must recognise that poor developing countries need adequate, reliable and affordable energy services to enable them to achieve acceptable living standards for their own citizens.

International co-operation can accelerate and reduce the costs of the development and deployment of new, low-carbon technologies that will be essential to reduce our dependence on fossil fuels. In particular the UK will be working with International Financial Institutions (IFI) – such as the World Bank – to reduce market barriers to investment and increase development bank lending for low carbon technologies.

International energy and energy efficiency

The International Energy Strategy (2004) sets out how the Government proposes to meet the international challenge of maintaining access to secure and affordable energy supplies and mitigating the effects of climate change.

The Renewable Energy and Energy Efficiency Partnership (REEEP) is a global World Summit on Sustainable Development (WSSD) partnership for accelerating and expanding the global market for renewable energy and energy efficiency systems/technologies. It focuses on policy and regulation, and innovative financing in both the developed and the developing world, to raise awareness and to develop and spread best practice.

Photovoltaics initiative in Qinghai, China

---

[7] The International Energy Agency (2004) reported that 1.6 billion people, a quarter of the world's population, live without electricity and 2.4 billion people use only traditional biomass for their cooking and heating.

In December 2004, the UK Government committed an additional £2.5 million to REEEP for 2005/6. This is the largest commitment from any country so far and is in addition to the £1 million of new money already committed by the UK for 2005/6.

International Round Table

Defra and DTI are jointly hosting a Round Table in London (15-16 March 2005) to consider the challenge of achieving a sustainable and secure energy future for all in a lower carbon world between now and 2050. The Round Table will be attended by Energy and Environment ministers from around 20 countries with significant energy needs over the next 50 years, alongside selected senior figures from business and from the key multilateral organisations concerned with energy and environmental issues.

The Round Table will focus on the international drivers for how energy policy over the next 50 years can help deliver lower carbon economies. We intend to encourage a useful and informal dialogue on the policy frameworks needed to balance energy access, energy security and environmental concerns; and in particular, how the technological challenges and the potential financing mechanisms for lower carbon energy systems can be taken forward.

4. The UK policy framework

The UK Climate Change Programme (CCP) was published in 2000. It set out a package of policies to help achieve our Kyoto target and move us towards our national 2010 goal.

These policies included measures to promote energy efficiency in homes and businesses, introduce industry to the benefits of emissions trading, increase the share of electricity generated by renewable resources, encourage the take up of less polluting vehicles, and encourage individuals and communities to consider how to reduce carbon dioxide emissions for example through the work of the Energy Saving Trust.

Further developments since the publication of the Programme include:

> the Energy White Paper (2003) which established tackling climate change as one of the four goals for energy policy

> the EU emissions trading scheme, launched earlier this year

> the Energy Efficiency Action Plan (2004), and

> a requirement for Government to make carbon impact assessment an integral part of assessing the environmental impacts of new policies as part of the general Regulatory Impact Assessments (RIAs) that are completed before policies are implemented.

The Energy White Paper

The Government set out its strategy to address the challenges facing our energy system in 2003: 'Our energy future: creating a low carbon economy'. The White Paper provides a long-term framework for developing policies to ensure that UK has access to sustainable, reliable and affordable energy, through competitive markets. It sets out four goals for energy policy:

➤ to put ourselves on a path to cut the UK's carbon dioxide emissions – the main contributor to climate change – by some 60 per cent by about 2050, with real progress by 2020

➤ to maintain the reliability of energy supplies

➤ to promote competitive markets in the UK and beyond, helping to raise the rate of sustainable economic growth and to improve our productivity, and

➤ to ensure that every home is adequately and affordable heated.

The Government believes that these four goals can be achieved together. Energy efficiency is likely to be the cheapest and safest way of addressing all four objectives. Renewable energy will also play an important part in reducing carbon dioxide emissions, while also strengthening energy security and improving our industrial competitiveness as we develop cleaner technologies, products and processes.

Social costs of carbon emissions and policy-making

The Government is playing a key role in promoting research on the cost of inaction on climate change, including cutting-edge work aimed at deriving illustrative estimates of the social cost of carbon (SCC) for use in economic appraisal and cost-benefit analysis.

Deriving SCC estimates is very challenging. The models on which they are based are improving but still offer a rather coarse and incomplete picture of damage costs. There is also growing concern over the major potential impacts not included in the underlying modelling studies, not least abrupt climate changes and large-scale socio-economic effects in vulnerable regions or countries.

In January 2004 the Government commissioned two research projects aimed at improving the available SCC estimates, and to explore how they could be applied to policy assessment.

Policies to reduce emissions fall under six broad sectors:

➤ the energy supply industry
➤ business
➤ transport
➤ households
➤ agriculture, forestry and land use, and
➤ the public sector.

However, a number of policies and initiatives deliver across all sectors – for example the EU emissions trading scheme, the reform of building regulations, and our new Climate Change Communications Initiative.

In September 2004 the UK Government launched a review of the UK Climate Change Programme. The review is looking at how existing policies are performing and the range of policies that might be put in place in the future to further reduce greenhouse gases and carbon dioxide emissions.

> ▶ **The Government is aiming to launch the revised UK Climate Change Programme in summer 2005**

The six key sectors

i. Energy supply

The future development of the energy supply sector is crucial to the UK's ability to meet its greenhouse gas and carbon dioxide emission goals.

The Renewables Obligation, launched in April 2002, requires electricity suppliers to source a percentage of their electricity sales from eligible renewable sources. The current target is for 10 per cent of electricity to be supplied from renewables by 2010/11, with an aspiration to double this by 2020. The Government has also announced its intention to extend the obligation to 15 per cent in 2015/16.

> ▶ **A statutory consultation on proposed changes to the Obligation will be published in summer 2005, with a view to any resulting changes to legislation coming into force on 1 April 2006**

The Government is also committed to investigating the contribution that renewable heat sources such as 'biomass' – energy products derived from wood and specially grown crops – can make.

> ▶ **A scoping study on the heat market, likely carbon savings and how to best help deliver the benefits will be published later in 2005**

Combined Heat and Power[8] (CHP) is a potentially more efficient form of energy supply that provides heat and electricity at the same time. The Government has set a target of achieving at least 10 gigawatts (GW) of 'Good Quality CHP capacity', i.e. capacity that meets or exceeds set standards, by 2010. In 2004, the Government published a strategy for Combined Heat and Power to 2010, which set out a framework to support the growth of Good Quality CHP capacity.

The Energy White Paper set out a vision for 2020 that includes much more diverse, local electricity generation with different micro-generation technologies, supplying the needs of individual consumers and buildings, and providing excess electricity back into the National Grid. Initial discussions have already taken place with the micro-generation industry.

> ▶ **A consultation on a strategy to promote micro-generation will be launched in 2005.**

---

[8] CHP is technology that offers significant energy efficiency and environmental benefits relative to comparable, separate, conventional methods of heat and power generation.

The long-term potential of carbon capture and storage (CCS) technologies, which capture carbon dioxide from fossil fuel fired power stations and other very large energy users and stores them, was also recognised in the Energy White Paper. The UK Government is currently developing a Carbon Abatement Technology (CAT) Strategy. This will include a target for bringing new CCS technologies to the market by 2020.

➤ **The Carbon Abatement Technology Strategy is to be published in 2005**

The Energy White Paper made it clear that, in reducing carbon dioxide emissions, our priority is to strengthen the contribution of energy efficiency and renewable energy courses. Nuclear power is currently an important source of carbon-free electricity. Its current economics, however, make it an unattractive option for new capacity. There are also important issues to be resolved in relation to managing nuclear waste. With this in mind, the White Paper did not include specific proposals for building new nuclear power stations. We do not rule out the possibility that, at some point in the future, new nuclear build might be necessary if we are to meet our emission reduction goals. Before any decision to build new stations, there would need to be a full public consultation and the publication of a further white paper setting out our proposals.

ii. Business

Business commitment to tackling climate change is growing in the UK. Tackling climate change can bring wide-ranging benefits including lower costs, improved competitiveness and new market opportunities. The policy framework for the business sector recognises its diversity and the fact that some areas will find it easier to respond to climate change than others. It also recognises that some industry sectors are much bigger emitters than others, and is structured to get the biggest emitters on board first.

Policies for this sector are primarily focused on reducing carbon dioxide emissions by improving industrial energy efficiency. Business greenhouse gas emissions have fallen since 1990, and by 2010 are projected to have fallen by about 26 per cent from their 1990 levels.

The **climate change levy** (CCL) was introduced in 2001 as a tax on the business use of energy providing an incentive to cut usage. **Climate change agreements** were introduced at the same time. Under the agreements, energy intensive sectors covered by the levy – such as steel manufacturing – were given the opportunity to sign up to 10-year negotiated agreements covering energy use and/or emission reductions in return for an 80 per cent discount on the climate change levy. There are currently 44 sectors with over 10 000 sites covered by the agreements. Significant carbon savings have already been made and some sectors have already achieved their 2010 targets. Following consultation with business, in the Budget 2004, the Government announced that the negotiated agreements would be extended to those sectors that pass an energy intensity threshold, and can in some cases demonstrate the existence of international competition issues.

➤ **The Government is awaiting State Aids approval from the European Commission and foresees the new sectors entering for the agreements during 2005**

The Carbon Trust

The Carbon Trust was launched in 2002, to help the implementation of energy efficiency in the business and public sectors as well as encourage the development of a low carbon sector in the UK. It operates the UK's main information, advice and research programme for organisations in the public and private sectors. Its programmes includes the Carbon Management Programme to support UK organisations as they begin to make the risks and opportunities presented by climate change as part of their core activities. It also administers and promotes the Energy Technology List of energy efficient technologies eligible for 100 per cent first year capital allowances under the Enhanced Capital Allowances Scheme.

Over the next three years the Government will invest at least £192 million in the Carbon Trust's programmes to meet growing demand for their services, and develop existing programmes. In the 2004 Pre-Budget Report, the Chancellor announced a new £20 million fund, to be managed by the Carbon Trust, to accelerate the development and use of energy-efficient technologies.

A key tool for reducing greenhouse gas emissions is emissions trading.

The **UK emissions trading scheme** (UK ETS) is a voluntary scheme which aims to provide cost-effective emissions reductions and to give UK businesses a head start in emissions trading, before future international trading schemes begin to take force. At an auction in 2002, organisations bid emissions reductions over five years to 2006 in return for a share of incentive money. Participants have committed to reduce their baseline emissions by 11.88 million tonnes of carbon dioxide equivalent over the life of the scheme. A further 8.9 million tonnes of carbon dioxide equivalent emissions reductions have been pledged by six participants who have significantly exceeded targets in the first two years. Through the CCP review the Government will be examining the potential for continuing with the scheme beyond 2006 and whether there is any scope for extending it.

The **EU emissions trading scheme** (EU ETS), introduced in January 2005, is a key component of the EU's drive to reduce emissions of greenhouse gases. The Government's approach to the EU ETS aims to balance the achievements of our environmental goals with the need for a stable supply of energy and the need to ensure the competitiveness of industry in the international market. We believe that the Scheme should be a central plank of the UK's future emission reduction policy.

The UK is showing its commitment to the scheme by setting a cap on allowances in the first phase (2005-2007) that takes us beyond our Kyoto emissions target. A second phase of the EU ETS will commence in 2008 and run until 2012 to coincide with the Kyoto commitment period; all member States will be required to use the scheme to contribute to meeting their part of the EU's shared Kyoto target.

The Government is at the early stage of developing its approach to phase II, but is aware that business is keen for early certainty about its plans for implementation. Through the review of the CCP we are giving consideration to the extent to which we can do this.

How emissions trading works

Emissions trading involves buying and selling emissions "allowances", measured in units equivalent to tonnes of carbon dioxide. Every year, each participant is allocated a set number of allowances, which may be traded within the community. At the end of each year, the participant must report their annual emissions. If there are insufficient allowances in that participant's account to cover their emissions, then they are liable to financial penalties.

If a participant reduces their emissions below their allowance, they can keep the surplus for use in future years or sell it. Alternatively, they can buy extra allowances to cover any shortfall. Emissions trading therefore provides an incentive for participants to reduce their emissions since they can sell the surplus to others and make a profit.

The introduction of the EU ETS means that overlapping policy measures cover some business sector emissions. Therefore the future mix of measures impacting on business is being considered as part of the CCP review.

In addition to trading greenhouse gas emissions, the Government believes that there is potential to introduce trading into the energy efficiency arena. This is known as **white certificate trading**. The proposed Energy Use Efficiency and Energy Services Directive would create a framework in which such a scheme could be considered at European level. However, there are many issues that would need careful consideration, including the monitoring and verification of efficiency gains and the establishment of baselines from which to measure improvement.

> ❯ **The UK Government is committed to assessing the part such a scheme could play by 2007**

How white certificate trading works

"White certificate" refers to the concept of a tradable commodity that represents an amount of saved energy, or avoided energy use. Companies would be set a target level of energy efficiency improvement, and could meet this by either increasing their energy efficiency or by buying certificates from other participants who had generated a surplus.

The waste management process also emits greenhouse gases, predominately methane. Landfill emissions in the UK are falling, mainly because more landfill gas is collected for energy recovery and environmental control. There are also a number of Government policies to reduce biodegradable waste being disposed of in landfill sites, e.g. increases in landfill tax.

The European Community's Landfill Directive will have a significant effect on emissions by imposing strict engineering requirements on landfill sites, by requiring that gas from these sites is captured, and by imposing limits on the amount of biodegradable municipal waste taken to landfill sites.

> **A Landfill Allowances Trading Scheme will be introduced in England from 1 April 2005 to help local authorities to restrict the amount of biodegradable municipal waste landfilled to ensure that the UK's target under the Directive is met**

iii. Transport

The Government recognises that transport has to make a contribution to reducing carbon dioxide emissions. The transport sector – excluding international aviation – is currently responsible for about a quarter of total UK carbon dioxide emissions, 80 per cent of this is contributed by road users. The contribution to total UK carbon dioxide emissions from domestic transport is expected to remain broadly stable to 2020 as emissions from other sectors are forecast to fall.

The **Future of Transport White Paper (2004)**[9] recognises that we need to ensure that we can benefit from mobility and access while minimising the impact on other people and the environment. It notes that to ensure that transport makes its full contribution to reducing carbon dioxide emissions cost-effectively, we need to broaden the debate on the:

> value we attach to the movement of people and goods

> overall price of transport, and

> costs of reducing carbon across all sectors of the economy.

There are a number of ways in which the Government is addressing the need to reduce carbon dioxide and other emissions from the **road transport sector**:

Fiscal incentives

Fiscal incentives have successfully promoted a switch to less polluting main fuels, while promoting the growth of alternative fuels. Key successes have been:

> delivery of ultra-low sulphur petrol and diesel through duty differentials

> using duty to encourage development of the LPG market – with sales above 200m litres a year, and

> using incentives to develop biofuels market share.

Both the Company Car Tax and Vehicle Excise Duty regimes have been reformed to link directly to the emissions profile of vehicles. The change to the Company Car Tax regime are expected to contribute between 0.5–1.0 million tonnes of carbon savings per year in the medium term.

The **Powering Future Vehicles (PFV) Strategy,**[10] launched in July 2002, provides a framework for shifting the UK vehicle market to clean, low-carbon vehicles and fuels. Implementation has included:

> grant incentives for cleaner and more fuel efficient vehicles

> building on the existing fuel duty incentives to support the introduction of low carbon fuels, and

---

[9] See www.dft.gov.uk/stellent/group/dft_about/documents/divisionhomepage/031259.hcsp
[10] See www.dft.gov.uk/stellent/group/dft_roads/documents/dft_roads_506885.hcsp

➤ funding of research, development and demonstrations to promote efficient vehicles and low carbon fuel technologies.

The Pre-Budget Report in December also announced a feasibility study and consultative process on a possible Renewable Transport Fuels Obligation.

The **Low Carbon Vehicle Partnership**[11], set up as part of the PFV Strategy was instrumental in developing a voluntary colour-coded energy efficiency label for new cars – similar to those now used for white goods (large domestic appliances) – to provide consumers with clear, simple information about the climate change impacts of different vehicle makes and models. The Government launched this label in February 2005.

➤ **The label is due to be in all UK car showrooms by September 2005**

Voluntary agreements between the European Commission and the automotive industry commit car manufacturers to improve fuel efficiency of new cars sold in the EU by 25 per cent between 1995 and 2008/9.

➤ **We are pressing the European Commission to finalise a new round of voluntary agreements on new car fuel efficiency with the industry**

Dawn traffic on the M25
Source: *Martin Bond/Still Pictures*

Government car fleet procurement currently has a target for 10 per cent of cars to be alternatively fuelled by March 2006. This technology based definition is no longer viable as it does not account for emissions improvement in the diesel sector. For the future, Government will procure on an emissions (not technology) basis, and within the review of the Sustainable Development in Government (SDiG) Framework we will develop a commitment to ensure that Government only procures the cleanest vehicles.

The DfT Powering Future Vehicles Strategy set a target that by 2012, 10 per cent of all new cars sold would be defined as low carbon[12].

➤ **The Government will take this forward with the intention that 10 per cent of all of its vehicles will be low carbon by 2012**

The UK **aviation sector**[13] contributed about 5.5 per cent of the UK's carbon dioxide emissions in 2000, and as a result of radiative forcing[14] (RF) 11 per cent of the total UK climate change impact. The future growth in air transport could mean that the aviation sector contributes between 33-35 per cent of the total UK climate change impact by 2050, assuming all other sectors meet the targets set out in the Energy White Paper.[15]

[11] See www.lowcvp.org.uk
[12] Defined as CO_2 emissions of 100g/km or less at the tailpipe.
[13] All domestic services plus all international departures from the UK combined were estimated to contribute this amount.
[14] Radiative Forcing (RF) reflects aircraft-induced climate change caused by all emissions, not just the contribution from the release of fossil carbon alone.
[15] Environmental Audit Committee report, 'Aviation: Sustainability and the Government's second response'.

> ▶ **The Future of Air Transport White Paper (2003) includes a commitment to press for the inclusion of intra-EU air services in the EU emissions trading scheme**

Commercial air travel is a truly global industry, where many of the larger suppliers operate across all continents, and customers can switch suppliers quickly and easily. An international emissions trading regime is, therefore, the best solution. The UK Government is pressing for the development and implementation of such a regime, through the International Civil Aviation Organisation (ICAO).

A top priority for the UK's Presidency of the EU is to pave the way for aviation joining the EU emissions trading scheme by 2008 (or as soon as possible thereafter) as the UK believes that emissions trading represents the most effective economic instrument to tackle the climate change impacts of aviation[16]. But we recognise that it may not provide a total solution. So the Government will also continue to explore the use of other economic instruments building on the work in the joint DfT/HM Treasury report from March 2003 'Aviation and the Environment: Using Economic Instruments'.

The Government is encouraging the industry as it develops its commercial aviation sustainability strategy which is due to be launched later this year. The strategy includes all sectors of the industry – mainly manufacturers, airlines and airports – and is intended to set goals with milestones and deliverables. The Government expects the industry to use this opportunity to take a meaningful step forward on the path towards sustainability.

iv. Households and energy efficiency

The Government has introduced a range of measures to stimulate take-up of energy efficiency measures in the home, as well as in business. These include regulatory and incentive-based policies, grants and other economic incentives, and the provision of information and advice. This information offers a starting point for the wider community action on climate change supported through Community Action 2002 – Together We Can.

Energy Efficiency: The Government's Plan for Action was published in April 2004, setting out a clear framework for improving energy efficiency at an unprecedented level, with a particular focus to 2010. The Action Plan sets out a detailed implementation plan that will save over 12 million tonnes of carbon per year by 2010 – more than half the UK's overall carbon saving target for 2010. This is 20 per cent more than we thought was possible at the time of the White Paper and will save businesses and households over £3 billion per year on their energy bills.

Key measures include the intention to double the level of Energy Efficiency Commitment activity from 2005 to 2011 subject to a review in 2007, improving the energy standards of buildings through revisions to the Building Regulations, an additional £140m for tackling fuel poverty in England, including through 'Warm Front', over the period 2005-08, additional economic incentives for energy efficiency, announced in the 2004 budget, including tax relief for landlords installing insulation, and new energy services pilots.

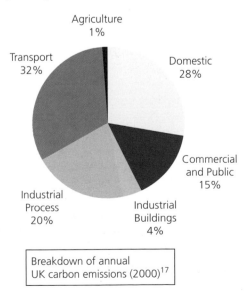

Breakdown of annual UK carbon emissions (2000)[17]

Agriculture 1%
Transport 32%
Domestic 28%
Commercial and Public 15%
Industrial Process 20%
Industrial Buildings 4%

---

[16] The European Commission has instituted a study to look in detail at how emissions trading for aviation could work. This will report in summer 2005, coinciding with the UK's presidency of the EU.

[17] BRE, 2003, 'Carbon dioxide emissions from non-domestic buildings 2000 and beyond.'

> **The Government is committed to raising the average energy efficiency of domestic homes by a fifth by 2010 compared to 2000**

The improvements to the energy standards of new homes will collectively deliver a reduction in carbon emissions of 1.4 million tonnes each year.

The Energy Performance of Buildings Directive requires Member States to set minimum requirements on the energy performance of new buildings and of large buildings undergoing major renovation, and the certification of all buildings at the point of sale and rental, within the European Community.

> **The Government is committed to implement this Directive by 2006**

The current provisions of Part L of the Building Regulations, which came into effect in 2002, are expected to deliver significant carbon savings to 2010.

> **A further revision of Part L of the Building Regulations will be released in 2005 delivering about a 25 per cent increase in energy efficiency in new buildings, and greatly extending the impact on energy efficiency of existing buildings**

> **Between 2010 and 2020, the Government aims to update the Building Regulations every five years or so with each stage signalling what the next stage is likely to be. This should lead to incremental increases in the energy standards of new and refurbished buildings**

The Sustainable and Secure Buildings Act (passed in 2004) will allow building regulations to address the sustainability of new buildings as well as to address conservation of fuel and power, or prevention or reduction of greenhouse gas emissions in relation to existing buildings.

> **The Government is now working with the Sustainable Development Commission to explore how these new powers might be applied most effectively. The Sustainable Development Commission is researching the techniques, costs, benefits and support mechanisms necessary to improve the resource efficiency of the existing building stock**

The Government is developing with industry a **Code for Sustainable Buildings**. This will establish stretching voluntary standards for resource efficiency on key issues such as energy, water, waste and materials, which could collectively deliver significant carbon savings. The Code will encourage builders to go beyond the letter of the regulations and minimise resource use from the start, and will be updated as technology develops. The Code is being developed to apply to all new buildings, with the focus initially on new housing stock. In due course the Government's aim is to apply the Code also to major refurbishments of existing housing stock. An initial outline of the Code was produced at the end of January 2005.

> **The Government intends to consult on the Code during 2005, including full-scale practical demonstrations of how the Code will be applied in a range of locations including the Thames Gateway. National rollout is planned to begin in 2006**

> ❯ **Where the Government is engaged in public-private partnerships to develop sites we will ensure that these higher standards are applied to all new homes**

Energy saving materials, components and appliances are being promoted through labeling schemes and financial incentives. Potential energy savings are offered by Micro-CHP (mCHP) and heat pump technologies. Micro-CHP provides the simultaneous generation of carbon efficient heat and electricity in a unit about the same size as a domestic boiler. Heat pumps use ambient heat (sourced from the ground, water or even the air) to quadruple the heating potential of electricity.

> ❯ **The 2004 Budget introduced a reduced rate of VAT on mCHP from 2005, subject to trials, and reduced rate VAT on ground source heat pumps, a viable carbon efficient means of heating for buildings that are off the gas grid**

The Energy Saving Trust

The Energy Saving Trust is a private, non-profit organisation, funded by Defra, DTI, DfT, the devolved administrations and the private sector. It has two major activities directed at households: running a network of 52 Energy Efficiency Advice Centres to provide advice for consumers and local authorities; and an Energy Efficiency campaign to encourage consumers to reduce their energy use and install energy efficiency devices.

In addition, the Major Photovoltaic Demonstration Programme (run by EST, funded by DTI) grant funds innovative use of photovoltaic installations, for domestic and non-domestic buildings. And the Community Energy Programme (run by EST and the Carbon Trust), grant funds the installation of district/community heating systems. Where these are not carbon neutral in the first instance, the valuable infrastructure investment will allow CHP/biomass plant to be used for wide scale carbon efficient heating and cooling in the medium term.

> ❯ **The Government has allocated an additional £10 million to EST for 2005-2008 to extend the Community Energy Programme.**

As part of the **Decent Homes** programme the Government is committed to ensuring that amongst other things, all social homes (i.e. those owned by local authorities or Housing Associations) have effective insulation and heating by 2010. 'Decent Homes' guidance also encourages landlords to carry out further energy efficiency measures when working on their properties. For the private sector, the new landlord's energy saving allowance, announced in the 2004 Budget will encourage private landlords to invest in the insulation of their properties.

BedZed – an innovative eco-friendly estate, Wallington, Surrey

v. Land Use, Agriculture and Forestry

The land use planning system provides the key framework for managing development and the use of land in ways which take into account the sustainable use of our natural resources; for example, by promoting or encouraging the use of renewable energy in new developments and reducing the use of non-renewable resources (and emissions) by locating development where it can be accessed by means other than by private car. The Government's new planning policy statement 'Delivering Sustainable Development' (PPS 1) sets out our vision for planning and the key policies which will underpin it. This is described in detail in the section between chapters 5 and 6.

Agricultural processes both emit and absorb greenhouse gases. Carbon is absorbed from the atmosphere when forest coverage or the amount of organic matter in the soil increases. Emissions mainly result from animals' digestive processes, animal wastes, fertiliser use and a change in land use. There are few direct policies for reducing greenhouse gas emissions in this sector. However, many other policies lead to indirect reductions. These include reforms to the Common Agricultural Policy which separated payments to farmers from incentives for production, and made payments conditional on farmers meeting minimum environmental standards.

The **England Rural Development Programme** (ERDP) – which delivers the EU Rural Development Regulation (RDR) in England – tackles climate change directly through schemes such as the Energy Crops Scheme, and less directly through the agri-environment schemes. **Environmental Stewardship**, launched in March 2005, should also encourage activity that helps to reduce emissions.

The UK Government believes that future EU rural development policy should focus more effectively on key EU environmental priorities, including a contribution to climate change mitigation and adaptation. The new EU Rural Development Regulation (RDR) is currently being negotiated for the 2007-2013 period

Non-food crops can reduce emissions by being substituted for petrochemicals. Crop-derived fuels can substitute for transport fuels and biomass from crops can be used to generate heat and electricity. Crops can also be used to replace other petrochemical-based products, e.g. plastics. Support for planting non-food crops is available through the Energy Crops Scheme. The Bioenergy Infrastructure Scheme, launched last year, provides aid for supply chain development throughout the UK. However, growth in this area has so far been limited.

> **The Government has established a taskforce to analyse barriers to the development of energy crops and to make recommendations on the contribution of biomass, taking into account the implications for the rural economy and land use.**

Forestry practices can make a significant contribution by reducing greenhouse gas emissions through increasing the amount of carbon removed from the atmosphere by the national forest estate, by burning wood for fuel, and by using wood as a substitute for energy-intensive materials such as concrete and steel. There are a number of incentive schemes for planting trees that will help to reduce carbon emissions. These include the **Farm Woodland Premium Scheme** (part of the ERDP) that encourages tree planting on land currently in productive agriculture.

vi. Public Sector

The public sector has an important role to play in providing leadership and driving change in other sectors.

Under the **Framework for Sustainable Development on the Government Estate** there are a number of targets for central departments and their executive agencies relating to climate change, including:

> **Reducing absolute carbon emissions, from fuel and electricity used in buildings on their estate, by 12.5 per cent by 2010-11, relative to 1999-2000**

> **Increasing the energy efficiency of buildings on their estate by 15 per cent by 2010-11, relative to 1999-2000**

> **Sourcing at least 10 per cent of electricity from renewable sources by March 2008**

> **Sourcing at least 15 per cent of electricity from Good Quality CHP by 2010**

> **A new commitment by central Government to buy and rent buildings with energy peformance in the top 25 per cent**

> **The Government is also planning to develop a long-term strategy, up to 2020, for sourcing renewable energy on the Government Estate**

Pilot carbon offsetting scheme

Some businesses and individuals already take measures to 'offset' the carbon impacts of their air travel. While this is no substitute for policy action on aviation, the Government is already committed to offsetting the travel impacts of events around its EU and G8 Presidencies.

In 2005, Defra, DFID and FCO, who account for the majority of total government air travel, will work together to pilot offsetting carbon dioxide emissions from official air travel. This joint approach will begin with self-assessment of air travel emissions and the development of a coordinated approach to investing in suitable offsetting projects that counterbalance these emissions by removing or preventing the emission of an equivalent amount of greenhouse gases. DfT are assisting with the development of the scheme.

The carbon offsetting initiative will not detract from our wider emission reduction objectives, but should be viewed as a complementary interim measure for tackling climate change emissions from aviation on a voluntary basis.

As described earlier, the Government remains convinced that the UK's priority should be emissions reductions and that the best way of ensuring that aviation contributes towards the goal of climate stabilisation is through a well-designed emissions trading scheme.

The approach through **schools** is two-fold. The education sector is important in terms of the opportunities to inform young people about climate change, but also because it is responsible for 10 per cent of all carbon emissions from all commercial and public buildings.

" *Sustainable development will not just be a subject in the classroom: it will be in its bricks and mortar and the way the school uses and even generates its own power. Our students won't just be told about sustainable development, they will see and work within it: a living, learning, place in which to explore what a sustainable lifestyle means.*"

Prime Minister, September 2004

A whole school approach to energy efficiency is promoted through the Energy Efficiency Certification for School, and the Building Schools for the Future programme provides a valuable opportunity for increasing the efficiency of the school building stock. In addition, the Carbon Trust promotes the School Turnkey Energy Programme to encourage schools to implement an holistic approach to energy management.

❯ **The Government is working to develop an environmental assessment method for all new schools and major refurbishments and a framework for sustainable development for existing schools**

NHS Corporate Social Responsibility Programme

The NHS has the largest property portfolio in Europe and emits around 1 million tonnes of carbon from its energy usage alone. The NHS has two targets in England:

❯ to reduce the level of primary energy consumption by 15 per cent by 2010, compared to 2000 levels, and

❯ to achieve a target of 35-55 Gj/100m^3 energy efficiency performance for the healthcare estate for all new capital developments and major redevelopments or refurbishments; and that all existing facilities should achieve a target of 55-65 Gj/100m^3.

To help achieve these targets the Department of Health is currently finalising an energy carbon guide for the NHS in England. In addition, each NHS trust is already required to assess its environmental performance using the NHS Environmental Assessment Tool (NEAT).

These actions all form part of the NHS Corporate Social Responsibility Programme showing how, as this country's biggest employer, it can make a significant contribution to the health and sustainability of the communities it serves[18].

Further details on public procurement are given in Chapters 3 and 7.

Climate Change Communications Initiative (CCCI)

CCCI is designed to address public awareness of and attitudes towards climate change. Key attitudes include recognition that climate change is a here and now issue, that action starts with each individual, and that climate change represents an opportunity as well as a threat, as well as improving understanding of the causes and effects of climate change.

This initiative is intended to complement the more focused behaviour-change campaigns, such as those on energy efficiency led by the Energy Saving and Carbon Trusts. As part of Community Action 2020 – Together We Can, the initiative will focus strongly on communicating at a local and regional level, where the evidence suggests it can be most effective. The Government will establish a new fund, starting next financial year, to support climate change communications at a regional and local level.

[18] See DH, 2004, 'Choosing Health: making healthier choices easier', TSO.

> **The Government launched the Climate Change Communications Initiative in February 2005, confirming supporting funding of £12 million over the period 2005-2008**

5. Adaptation to climate change

Our past and present emissions of greenhouse gases and the slow response of the climate system, mean that some change is already inevitable. The climate change we experience over the next three decades or so is already largely determined, irrespective of how we now reduce our emissions. So we need to understand the unavoidable impacts, on the environment, on communities, and on businesses, so that we can prepare for them, both to reduce risks and to seize opportunities.

Adapting to these impacts may involve difficult decisions and significant investment, and decisions will have to accommodate inherent uncertainties about the nature of climate change. Adaption must be brought in to all aspects of sustainable development and climate change has been considered in relation to each aspect of this strategy.

Defra funds the UK Climate Impacts Programme (UKCIP) to help public and private stakeholders assess their vulnerability to climate impacts, so that they can develop their own responses. There are four areas of focus: to develop a national picture of impacts; to provide an interface between research and stakeholders; to support stakeholders in steps towards adapting and to promote best practice.

Scenarios of climate change

A sound understanding of the climate change that can be expected is needed to underpin how we choose to adapt. Scenarios of future climate change in the UK were published in 2002.

> **Over the next 2–3 years, this climate change scenario information will be revised, expanded and developed to meet stakeholder needs better**

Understanding the impacts of climate change

Stakeholder-led scoping studies (facilitated by UKCIP) investigating the impacts of climate change have been completed in all of the English regions and the Devolved Administrations. Detailed research has been carried out, or is underway, in a number of priority sectors, and by a number of organisations, particularly in the water resources and flood/coastal management sectors, but also including animal and plant diversity, agriculture, tourism/recreation/leisure, health, spatial planning and the built environment, and business.

> **A report to be published in 2005 will integrate findings from all UKCIP studies to provide a national picture of the impacts of climate change and emerging adaptation options as currently known**

Working with stakeholders

Action in adapting to climate change is frequently carried out at regional or local levels and by public and private sector stakeholder organisations. Regional climate change partnerships in 7 of the 9 English regions have been established over the past four years, involving Government Offices in the Regions, regional and local government representatives, the Environment Agency, and a range of wider stakeholders. These partnerships form a crucial focus for adaptation actions.

Co-ordination of effort both in Government and among stakeholders is now required to achieve a comprehensive and consistent response to climate change across the UK.

> **In 2005 the Government will launch an Adaptation Policy Framework.**

This Framework will draw together the adaptation policies and activities across Government. Public and private sector organisations at local, regional and national levels, including the new Integrated Agency and the Environment Agency, will be instrumental in delivering the actions identified under the Framework.

Adapting to reduce the increased risk of flooding

The Government is maintaining its substantial flood and coastal erosion risk management programme, including the building of better defences and improved flood warning. We have already introduced innovative approaches with the introduction of 'soft' flood defences and pro-actively managing the realignment of coastlines.

In autumn 2004, **The Making Space for Water** consultation exercise sought views on proposals for a new cross-Government strategy for England. This focuses on the sustainable management of flood and coastal erosion risk from all sources. A key priority is to reduce the risk of flooding to a greater proportion of vulnerable properties whilst making sure flood risk management policies across Government are forward looking, and contribute to sustainable development including biodiversity, water quality, urban drainage and regeneration. We intend to publish the new strategy in 2005.

Thames Flood Barrier

Vulnerable countries will need assistance in adapting to climate change impacts. The UK is working to mainstream climate change risks and impacts within development assistance and national development plans, and has funded studies on climate change in India, China and Africa. We are also planning to support country-led research in China, India and South Africa – to strengthen the capacity of key analysts and officials to develop proposals of their own. This will help ensure these countries are in a position to successfully integrate mitigation actions into their development plans, and help prepare them for future international negotiations on climate change.

> **Results of the UK Government's Africa study, announced at the Tenth Conference of the Parties to the UNFCCC Convention on Climate Change (COP 10), will support further policy development regarding working with African institutions and governments, and our G8 partners**

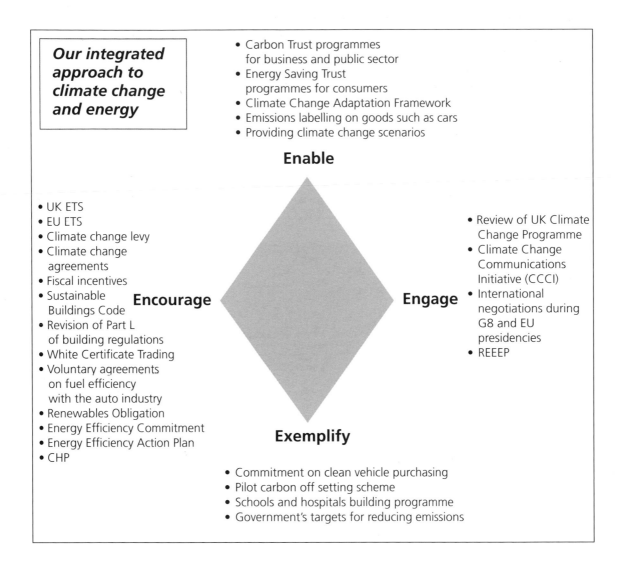

> **Our integrated approach to climate change and energy**

Enable
- Carbon Trust programmes for business and public sector
- Energy Saving Trust programmes for consumers
- Climate Change Adaptation Framework
- Emissions labelling on goods such as cars
- Providing climate change scenarios

Encourage
- UK ETS
- EU ETS
- Climate change levy
- Climate change agreements
- Fiscal incentives
- Sustainable Buildings Code
- Revision of Part L of building regulations
- White Certificate Trading
- Voluntary agreements on fuel efficiency with the auto industry
- Renewables Obligation
- Energy Efficiency Commitment
- Energy Efficiency Action Plan
- CHP

Engage
- Review of UK Climate Change Programme
- Climate Change Communications Initiative (CCCI)
- International negotiations during G8 and EU presidencies
- REEEP

Exemplify
- Commitment on clean vehicle purchasing
- Pilot carbon off setting scheme
- Schools and hospitals building programme
- Government's targets for reducing emissions

6. Measuring our progress

The indicators listed below include all indicators within the UK Framework set that are relevant to climate change and energy and in addition 'decoupling' (see Chapter 3) and other indicators relevant to the priorities of the UK Government Strategy.

Indicators to be used to report progress will include:

> **Greenhouse gas emissions***: Kyoto target and CO_2 emissions
> **CO_2 emissions by end user:** industry, domestic, transport (excluding international aviation), other
> **Aviation and shipping emissions:** greenhouse gases from UK-based international aviation and shipping fuel bunkers, and GDP
> **Renewable electricity:** renewable electricity generated as a percentage of total electricity

> **Energy supply:** UK primary energy supply and gross inland energy consumption
> **Electricity generation:** electricity generated, CO_2, NO_x and SO_2 emissions by electricity generators and GDP
> **Household energy use:** domestic CO_2 emissions and household final consumption expenditure
> **Road transport:** CO_2 emissions and GDP
> **Private vehicles:** CO_2 emissions and car-km and household final consumption expenditure
> **Road freight:** CO_2 emissions and tonne-km, tonnes and GDP
> **Manufacturing sector:** CO_2, emissions and GVA
> **Agriculture sector:** methane emissions and output
> **Service sector:** CO_2 emissions and GVA
> **Public sector:** CO_2 emissions and GVA

Note some indicators are relevant to other parts of the Strategy and are also listed in other chapters.

* Indicator is included in the UK Framework Indicators

Chapter 5
A Future Without Regrets: Protecting Our Natural Resources and Enhancing the Environment

The facts

➤ **72 per cent of the world's marine stocks are being harvested faster than they can reproduce**[1]

➤ **Some experts assess the rate at which species are becoming extinct at 1,000 to 10,000 times higher than the natural rate would be**[2]

➤ **Over 90% of the 1.2 billion people living in extreme poverty depend on forests for some part of their livelihoods**[3]. **Global forest cover decreased by 4% between 1990 and 2000**

➤ **Poorer communities tend to suffer the worst air quality – in England, the most deprived wards experience higher concentrations of pollution that harm human health. People in deprived wards are exposed to 41% higher concentrations of nitrogen dioxide than those people living in average wards**[4]

➤ **Activities within sectors that are closely and positively connected with the management of the natural environment support 299,000 full time equivalent jobs in England, and contribute £7.6 billion in gross value added**[5]

[1] Food and Agricultural Organisation's on-line statistical service at apps.fao.org
[2] European Commission 'Biodiversity loss: facts and figures' at europa.eu.int
[3] www.lnweb18.worldbank.org
[4] The Environment Agency.
[5] GHK Consulting Ltd, 2004, 'Revealing The Value Of The Natural Environment In England'.

Securing the future
delivering UK sustainable development strategy

Summary

Natural resources are vital to our existence and to the development of communities throughout the world.

The issues we face are the need for better understanding of environmental limits, the need for environmental enhancement where the environment is most degraded to ensure a decent environment for everyone, and the need for a more integrated policy framework to deliver this.

Taking it on consultation responses

In the 'Taking it on' consultation paper, natural resource issues were treated as a subset of the sustainable consumption and production priority. This was criticised by several respondents, who believed that natural resources deserved a much higher profile in the new strategy, one that encompassed the management as well as use of natural resources. The new strategy therefore makes protecting natural resources a separate priority. In response to the consultation and other feedback, the new sustainable development principles place living within environmental limits at the heart of the new strategy.

1. Our approach

Natural resources are vital to our existence. Our health and wellbeing are inextricably linked to the quality of our air, water, soils and biological resources. The use of their environmental wealth is vital for economic development and poverty reduction in this country and abroad. Our economy and key industrial sectors are directly and indirectly reliant on functioning ecosystems, which are vital for nutrient cycling, atmospheric and climate regulation, and break down and mitigation of waste. Our landscapes, seascapes and wildlife are inseparable from our culture and sense of identity. For many people the natural world has its own intrinsic value.

The demands made on natural resources continue to grow as people's desire to consume more is coupled with a rise in population. Here in the UK, one of the world's largest economies, we have high levels of consumption that are replicated throughout the developed world. Elsewhere, in less economically developed countries, economic growth is also driving rising consumption.

In the UK we know how to substantially reduce many of the traditional sources of pollution and we have made some important progress towards this e.g. organic pollution from sewage works, sulphur dioxide from power stations, chemicals from industry. The most serious problems that remain are more difficult to solve – they are chronic, diffuse and persistent – and they affect deprived communities disproportionately. If we are to tackle these issues effectively we need to adopt an ecosystems approach and develop our understanding of environmental limits described in this chapter.

We need consistent policies to protect and enhance those natural resources on which we depend. The development of links between individual policies in the context of the wider environment is key to our approach to the protection of natural resources as a whole. As a first step towards this more comprehensive approach:

▶ **The Government will work with stakeholders to develop a clear vision and coherent approach for the UK to the protection and enhancement of natural resources by the end of 2005**

There are three broad foundations on which we will build this new approach to protecting natural resources:

▶ developing the evidence base

▶ integrating policy, and

▶ tackling degraded resources and environmental inequalities.

What do we mean by natural resources?

Natural resources provide environmental services (e.g. nutrient cycling, climate and atmospheric regulation, and flood defence) and can be thought of in five overlapping ways.[6] Each of these reflect values that we associate with them:

Raw materials such as minerals and biomass – minerals such as sand, gravel and stone, fossil fuels, metal ores, gypsum and clay are non-renewable because they cannot be replenished within a human timescale.[7] In contrast, biomass is in principle renewable within the human timeframe, and includes quickly renewable resources, like agricultural crops and slowly renewable resources like timber. However, both of these can be pushed beyond their limits of recovery if over-exploited.

Environmental media such as air, water and soil – these resources sustain life and support biological resources on which we depend.

Flow resources such as wind, geothermal, tidal and solar energy – these resources cannot be depleted, but require other resources to exploit them. For example, energy, materials and space are needed to build wind turbines or solar cells.

Space is required to produce or sustain all the above – space provides land for our cities and towns, infrastructure, industry and agriculture. Wildlife, rivers and natural processes need it to function healthily.

Biological resources include dynamic ecosystems, species and genetic information – plants, animals and other organisms maintain the life-sustaining systems of the earth. Their variability (biodiversity) is also a resource and includes the diversity within species, between species and of ecosystems.

[6] Based on the EU document: 'Towards a thematic strategy on the sustainable use of natural resources', 2003.
[7] Chapter 3 addresses minerals resources.

Developing our vision for natural resources

There are already many policies, which aim to protect or enhance the environment. We need a clear long term vision to judge whether these policies add up. We have begun to develop a vision for the future, which reflects the new approaches and priorities emerging from our policies. Our work with stakeholders will include testing and developing this vision further:

> economic growth will no longer be confined to environmental degradation at home or abroad

> healthy and resilient terrestrial and marine ecosystems will be a clear indicator that we are managing multiple pressures from human activity appropriately and are conserving natural resources for future generations

> we will have clearly defined where environmental limits exist and have taken action to avoid breaching them

> the interdependence of environmental goals, particularly climate change, oceans and biodiversity will be widely recognised, and

> we will appreciate the fundamental dependence of human health and the global economy on a healthy environment.

In dealing with outputs of human activity which may have an impact on natural resources (e.g. emissions, waste, chemicals, GMOs), we are:

> taking an integrated approach to identify the causes of environmental degradation and acting to address problems as near to source as possible

> moving to tackle diffuse pollution as well as that from clearly identifiable sources, and

> integrating the precautionary principle – minimising the risk of harmful releases to the environment through better knowledge of potential impacts and better management.

2. Developing the evidence base

We need to consider ecosystems as a whole, taking into account social, economic and environmental objectives. To do this, we need a better understanding of how ecosystems work, their resilience and vulnerability, how they are affected by cumulative and combined pressures, and the value of ecosystem goods and services that they provide. This includes establishing where environmental limits exist.

The ecosystems approach

A focus on the health of ecosystems has emerged in recent years across marine, freshwater, biodiversity and soil policy. This shift signals a much more integrated approach to policy development. It caters for human as well as ecosystem wellbeing and enables us to consider conflicting objectives. It requires a precautionary approach, avoiding damage by putting in place measures to protect ecosystems before damage occurs, rather than trying to repair damage (which may be irreversible) after it has occurred.

The **Water Framework Directive** is an example of how we are moving towards an ecosystems approach. This legislation requires river basins to be managed as an entity to deliver good environmental outcomes in both surface and groundwater. For the first time ecological objectives are set for surface waters. We will be looking to those who use water and who may pollute it to contribute more fairly to the cost of achieving the

Directive's environmental objectives. This has implications for agriculture, land use and other activities, and will benefit from the work of partners. The Highways Agency, for example, has initiated long-term integrated water quality research aimed at developing an environmental assessment procedure compliant with the Water Framework Directive.

Working towards ecosystem-based management of natural resources means that we have to recognise that sustainable economic progress and better living standards are dependent on maintaining and enhancing natural resources. To do this, we will bring together our improved understanding of environmental limits and ensure that the true costs of the environment are taken into account in economic decisions.

Environmental limits

While resources such as biodiversity and soils are thought of as 'renewable', they can be exploited to the extent that long-term irreversible damage will be caused; hence the development of the concept of 'environmental limits'. Environmental limits are the level at which the environment is unable to accommodate a particular activity or rate of activities without sustaining unacceptable or irreversible change.

There is evidence that this is already occurring in many places, the commercial extinction of the Newfoundland cod fisheries being a notable example. Decisions that involve the sustainable use of natural resources need to take proper account of these limits so that suitable management measures can be put in place.

> **The Government will collate existing research and identify shortfalls in understanding about where environmental limits exist, and where they are being exceeded. We will then conduct a strategic assessment of future research needs in all policy areas.**

An early outcome from this work will be the development of protocols for monitoring sensitive environments.

These developments will complement existing research and monitoring initiatives led by the Government departments, agencies and research councils that provide up to date and reliable knowledge about the status of our resources. These include:

> the green spaces database which will bring together information on parks, allotments, city farms, playing fields and cemeteries, is being developed by the Office of the Deputy Prime Minister (ODPM)

> the 'Countryside Survey'[8] which looks at the condition of soils, vegetation, wildlife habitats and land cover

> the Environment Agency's 'State of the Environment Report'[9], and

> English Nature's reports on the 'State of Nature' in the Uplands, Lowlands and Maritime Environments, and on the condition of Sites of Special Scientific Interest (SSSI).[10]

[8] Defra, 2000, 'Countryside Survey' at www.defra.gov.uk/wildlife-countryside/cs2000/index.htm
[9] Environment Agency, 'State of the Environment Report' at www.environment-agency.gov.uk
[10] English Nature, State of Nature reports
  • 'Upland Challenge' at www.english-nature.org.uk/pubs/publication/pdf/wildnat.pdf
  • 'Future landscapes for wildlife' at www.english-nature.org.uk/pubs/publication/pdf/sonlow.pdf
  • 'Getting onto an even keel' at www.english-nature.org.uk/pubs/publication/pdf/sonmarsum.pdf
  • 'England's best wildlife and geological sites' at www.english-nature.org.uk/news/news_photo/SSSI_Condition_Report.pdf

To build on this material the Government will:

➤ **Undertake a new countryside survey in 2006 and 2007 to assess the status of natural resources in the UK countryside**

➤ **Publish a state of the seas report in March 2005**

➤ **Support work on the Global Biodiversity Outlook taking place under the Convention on Biological Diversity**

The UK holds some of the best information about natural resources available anywhere in the world. There are, however, still instances where decisions on managing natural resources will have to be taken on the basis of partial information. In these instances, and where, firstly, there is a risk of significant adverse environmental effects occurring and secondly, any possible mitigation measures seem unlikely to safeguard against these effects, the precautionary principle will be adopted. Where evidence exists of likely harm to ecosystems or biodiversity, we will adopt practices that avoid irreversible damage.

3. Integrating policy

Our commitments to protect natural resources are driven by a range of agreements, policy objectives and targets set at international, European and national levels. This policy framework is fragmented, complex and can give rise to conflicting priorities. To provide a more strategic approach to our actions we will tackle this fragmentation and move towards more integrated policy making.

We need to tackle both global and local pressures through international co-operation as well as action in the UK. At an international level this means taking a lead on protecting the global environment by working through institutions such as the UN. It also means supporting developing countries to integrate the principles of sustainable development into national policies and programmes.

In Europe we will work together with our partners on agricultural and environmental policy reforms.

In the UK there are a range of strategies to protect and enhance natural resources. These will be strengthened by new legislation for the marine environment and for common land, and by modernising our means of delivery.

Key international, European, and national policy commitments and new developments are listed in this chapter. More detailed summaries of the Government's environmental objectives have been compiled to facilitate understanding of the breadth of policies that contribute to sustainable development.

➤ **The updated and revised web resource www.sustainable-development.gov.uk sets out not only our indicators, and the targets for each of our policies, but the international, European and domestic policy and regulatory frameworks which supports the meeting of these targets**

Protecting the global environment

We are working to reverse the loss of environmental resources internationally by supporting multilateral environmental agencies. The United Nations, European Union and other international bodies, supported by funding mechanisms such as the Global Environmental Facility, provide the means to set and deliver environmental objectives across national boundaries. The delivery of these objectives requires environmental needs to be recognised in all policies: they cannot be considered in isolation.

The international policy framework

UN Conventions and other international agreements can set targets and have a potentially huge impact. They rely heavily on action at the national level to be effective. The UK is a signatory of many environmental conventions and agreements (the so called Multilateral Environmental Agreements) including those on:

> biological diversity (CBD)
> internationally traded endangered species (CITES)
> migratory species
> wetlands (RAMSAR)
> marine pollution (MARPOL)
> law of the sea (UNCLOS)
> climate change (Kyoto)
> long-range transboundary air pollution (CLRT AP)
> world heritage
> protection of the marine environment of the north east Atlantic (OSPAR)
> access to information, public participation in decision-making and access to justice in environmental matters (Aarhus)
> transboundary environmental impact assessment (Espoo)
> strategic environmental assessment (UNECE Protocol)
> persistent organic pollutants (Stockholm Convention)

Further guidance and advice comes through the United Nations Environment Programme (UNEP) and specialist agencies such as the Food and Agriculture Organisation (FAO). The FAO for example has developed International Action Plans such as those on seabirds, sharks and Illegal, Unregulated and Unreported (IUU) fishing, which fall under the Code of Conduct for Responsible Fisheries.

The UK is also committed to the UN Millennium Development Goals including ensuring environmental sustainability with a target of reducing the loss of environmental resources. Further commitments were agreed at the 2002 UN World Summit on Sustainable Development in Johannesburg. Our key international targets and commitments include:

> reduce significantly the current rate of biodiversity loss by 2010
> restore depleted fish stocks by 2015
> establish networks of marine protected areas by 2012
> halve proportion of people who do not have access to basic sanitation and water by 2015
> strengthen forest law enforcement and governance
> integrate principles of sustainable development into country policies and programmes

The United Nations Environment Programme (UNEP) is the principal strategic global environmental authority and the focal point for environmental action and co-ordination within the UN. The UK has been UNEP's largest single donor for the last two years, providing £4.2 million each year to its Environment Fund. The UK is a major contributor to the Convention on Biological Diversity, Montreal Protocol Fund, UN Convention to Combat Desertification and UN Forum on Forests. The UK also supports the Global

Environmental Facility, which provides grants to developing countries for projects that benefit the global environment and promote sustainable livelihoods.

> **The UK will support the call for a substantial replenishment of the Global Environmental Facility funding and promote continuing improvements to make it more streamlined – for speedier delivery of results for sustainable development**

While international agreements provide an agreed agenda, actions have to be taken within individual states. For the UK this includes working with its Overseas Territories, which are rich in natural resources and biodiversity, but in many cases are under threat. The Foreign and Commonwealth Office (FCO) and the Department for International Development (DFID) are jointly funding an Overseas Territories Environment Programme, worth £3 million up to 2006-07, to address this.

The Darwin Initiative draws on UK expertise in the area of biodiversity to fund collaborative projects forming partnerships with host countries. Since its launch in 1992 the Darwin Initiative has committed over £35 million to more than 350 biodiversity projects in 100 countries.

The Darwin Initiative

A community-driven conservation and ecotourism project led by the Durrell Institute of Conservation and Ecology, University of Kent has played a key role in the sustainable use of wildlife resources in the Mara region of Kenya.

Stephen Kisolu Darwin Scholar, courtesy of Matt Walpole

> **The UK will continue to promote biodiversity internationally through the Darwin Initiative, the Flagship Species Fund and the Global Opportunities Fund**

Illegal, Unregulated and Unreported (IUU) fishing is a worldwide problem. Levels of forgone revenues may be $20-30 billion each year. IUU fishing wreaks havoc on fish stocks and ecosystems. It carries a high social and economic cost borne disproportionately by poor people in developing countries from which over 50 per cent of internationally traded fishery products are derived.

> **The Government will promote international action to tackle IUU fishing through the FAO International Plan of Action, the Ministerial High Seas Task Force and other measures**

Forests

The UK supports the Forest Law Enforcement and Governance programme promoting regional initiatives in Africa and Asia to help developing countries strengthen their forest governance and trade. DFID is currently working on developing markets for watershed protection services. The UK has also played a major part in the development of the innovative EU Forest Law Enforcement Government and Trade Action Plan. This includes the development of a new EU regulation to prevent illegal timber from entering the European market.

Fifteen million people earn direct income from forests in Africa and more than 70 per cent of sub-Saharan Africa's population depends in large measure on forests and woodlands for livelihoods. Africa accounted for 56 per cent of global deforestation between 1990 and 2000[11].

[11] FAO, 2003, 'IEA World Energy Outlook 2003'.

Further actions by the UK to help address international biodiversity loss, sustain the marine environment and achieve sustainable fisheries are set out in more detail in the relevant 'World Summit on Sustainable Development Delivery Plans' published in May 2004[12].

Millennium Development Goal (MDG) 7 is to ensure environmental sustainability by integrating the principles of sustainable development into country policies and programmes, and by reversing the loss of environmental resources. The goal also includes targets for halving, by 2015, the proportion of people without access to safe drinking water and basic sanitation, and for improving the lives of 100 million slum dwellers by 2020.

This can best be achieved by countries defining their own development priorities and with international assistance to help manage resources sustainably. Poverty Reduction Strategies (PRSs) or equivalent national planning processes, which promote environmental sustainability, will be more effective at eradicating poverty[13]. However, World Bank monitoring and assessments reveal that more needs to be done to address environmental opportunities and risks in national PRS processes.

> **The Government will work to ensure environmental opportunities as well as risks, are reflected in Poverty Reduction Strategies and national development plans and will actively encourage all donors to do likewise**

The Government will also work to ensure water and sanitation are given appropriate emphasis in PRSs. DFID's 'Water Action Plan'[14] sets out how we plan to contribute to the achievement of the MDG target on water and sanitation.

The Commission for Africa

Africa's biodiversity is a key part of its comparative advantage for tourism and also for pharmaceuticals. Some 20,000 species are used in traditional medicine, forming the basis of primary health care for around 75 per cent of the population.

The importance of policies to promote sustainable economic growth and to strengthen the ability of poor people to participate fully in that growth will be highlighted in the forthcoming report from the Commission for Africa due in March 2005. It will recommend that environmental considerations should be integral to donor interventions by the end of 2006 and will encourage the inclusion of environmental sustainability into country-owned Poverty Reduction Strategies.

The Commission for Africa was established in February 2004 to provide a coherent set of policies to accelerate progress towards a strong and prosperous Africa. Other areas to be addressed in the report include mitigation of and adaptation to climate change; increased aid for water supply and sanitation; and measures to tackle illegal logging and improve natural resource revenue management.

---

[12] www.sustainable-development.gov.uk/wssd2/08.htm

[13] Interim or full poverty reduction strategies have been developed in 53 countries – see www.sustainable-development.gov.uk/taking-it-on/taskforce/sdtf6-0715-3.htm

[14] DFID, 2004, 'Water Action Plan' at www.dfid.gov.uk/pubs/files/wateractionplan.pdf to be updated in 2005 following the 13th session of the UN Commission on Sustainable Development which is focusing on water and sanitation goals, at www.un.org/esa/sustdev/csd/csd.htm.

European policy

The European policy framework

Much UK legislation on the environment derives from EU Directives. These cover air quality, noise, birds, habitats, environmental assessment and protection, water and waste. Many of these Directives include national targets. For example the Water Framework Directive has targets to:

> publish river basin management plans by 2009, and

> deliver 'good ecological quality' status for all inland and coastal waters by 2015

Projects affecting the environment are subject to the Environmental Impact Assessment (EIA) Directive while under the Strategic Environmental Assessment Directive (SEA) the effects of a wide range of plans and programmes must be established and taken into account in decision-making. The Office of the Deputy Prime Minister provides a range of guidance on EIA and SEA on its website.[15]

The UK is bound by agreements at the European level such as the European commitment to the UN Aarhus Convention and the World Trade Organisation. Agriculture and fisheries policy are subject to common EU policies where we actively negotiate reforms designed to achieve more sustainable outcomes. The EU also produces frameworks and guidance for national environmental policy that are agreed by member states and draw on EU and UN guidance. These include the EU Sustainable Development Strategy launched at the Gothenburg Summit in 2001, which committed the EU to halting the rate of biodiversity loss by 2010.

The EU's 6th Environment Action Programme (EAP), which runs until 2012, is the key framework for EU environmental policy development, setting objectives under four priority headings (climate change, nature and biodiversity, environment and health and quality of life, natural resources and waste). Sustainable development is a key principle of the 6th EAP. Equally, the 6th EAP indicates priorities for the environmental dimension of the EU Sustainable Development Strategy. The UK will be working to ensure that strategies and policies developed under the 6th EAP help deliver the EU sustainable development strategy and the UK sustainable development strategy.

An important set of frameworks being developed by the European Commission in 2005 under the 6th EAP are the seven Thematic Strategies (air quality, soil, sustainable use of resources, waste prevention and recycling, marine environment, urban environment and pesticides). They will set out a strategic, outcome-based approach to provide long-term direction in these important areas of EU environmental policy and will be tools for taking forward the sustainability agenda.

During its EU Presidency, the UK will seek to engage EU Ministers in strategic discussions on the thematic strategies and take forward the inherited environmental agenda. Specific objectives for the UK Presidency include:

> maintaining the EU's international leadership on climate change; specifically, taking forward discussions on extending the Emissions Trading Scheme to aviation and on the EU mandate for UN negotiations on post-Kyoto action

> reaching first stage agreement on a Chemicals Regulation (REACH) ensuring that benefits to health and the environment are properly balanced with competitiveness considerations

> taking forward proposals for a new directive on air quality standards, and

[15] www.odpm.gov.uk

> promoting sustainable consumption and production, and our climate change objectives, through concrete progress on green public procurement, so as to stimulate innovation and markets for environmental technologies and products.

Farming, food and fisheries – a special case and a new approach

The Government's Sustainable Farming and Food Strategy (2003) outlines a vision for agriculture in England that supports healthy and prosperous communities and a profitable and competitive industry while respecting the biological limits of natural resources. The Government is working with the devolved administrations and stakeholders to develop a sustainable fisheries policy building upon the Prime Minister's Strategy Unit report on the future of the fishing industry 'Net Benefits'.

Reforms to the Common Fisheries Policy (CFP), agreed in 2002, provide the tools for sustainable management of fisheries, including plans to recover depleted stocks; new Regional Advisory Councils to provide more stakeholder led and regionally focused management, and a new framework for fisheries agreements with non-EU countries.

Under new Common Agricultural Policy (CAP) arrangements, farmers will have greater freedom to respond to market demands, as the link between subsidies and production is broken. This provides better value for money for the taxpayer by reducing the incentive to overproduce and damage the environment, as well as significantly reducing the burden of bureaucracy on farmers. But new rules now require all applicants to keep land in good agricultural and environmental condition and observe certain requirements included in statutory management requirements as a condition of payment.

There are still areas, notably sugar and dairy, where artificially high prices, production quotas or other trade distorting measures remain in place. In the context of the Doha Development Agenda, high EU and other developed country tariff barriers need to be cut and market access improved across the board, particularly for the benefit of developing countries.

> **The Government will continue to seek further reform of the CAP, in particular to reform the sugar regime, to improve its wider public benefits and to cut costs. Within the World Trade Organisation it will work to secure agriculture agreement that reduces production subsidies, improves market access and eliminates export support**

> **The Government will build on CFP reforms by developing greater regionalisation, increased stakeholder participation, applying an ecosystems-based approach and integrating fisheries management more closely into management of the marine environment as a whole**

The national approach

In the UK, the Department of Environment, Food and Rural Affairs (Defra) leads on natural resource protection and enhancement. Defra works closely with the Office of the Deputy Prime Minister (ODPM) on issues such as land use planning and cleaner, safer and greener communities; ODPM and the Department for Trade and Industry on issues such as mineral extraction, energy and trade, and the Department for Transport on sustainable transport solutions. The Government has developed a number of strategies that address the pressures on natural resources as outlined below.

The policy framework in the UK

The following national statements of key Government objectives for the environment set out how to deliver statutory responsibilities, some of which draw on draw on UN and EU guidance[16]:

▶ The 'Air Quality Strategy 2000' for England, Wales, Scotland and Northern Ireland and its 2003 Addendum set demanding targets for nine key pollutants for protection of human health and two targets for ecosystem protection

▶ The Biodiversity Strategy for England 'Working with the Grain of Nature' sets out a programme which will integrate biodiversity into policy making and practice, in particular on agriculture, water, woodland, marine and coastal management, and urban issues

▶ The 'First Soil Action Plan for England: 2004-2006' is the first part of a programme aimed at embedding soil management in the natural resource protection agenda

▶ 'Directing the Flow – priorities for future water policy' sets future priorities for water policy in England. And we are consulting on a new cross-Government strategy for Flood risk management, Making Space for Water, which we intend to publish in Spring 2005

▶ Land management is a core aspect of England's Strategy for Sustainable Farming and Food 'Facing the Future'

▶ Policies for landscape conservation and enhancement, and improving recreational opportunities are contained in the White Paper 'Our Countryside: the future'

▶ The Marine Stewardship Report 'Safeguarding Our Seas' sets out a strategy for the conservation and sustainable development of our marine environment. We will also build on recent fundamental reviews, including the report of the Prime Minister's Strategy Unit 'Net Benefits – a sustainable and profitable future for the UK fishing industry', the Bradley Review of Marine Fisheries and Environmental Enforcement, the Review of Marine Nature Conservation, the Royal Commission on Environmental Pollution report 'Turning the Tide' on the impact of marine fisheries on the environment, and the Review of Development in Coastal and Marine Waters

▶ Planning Policy Statements provide the framework for regional and local land use planning in the English regions. Regional Spatial Strategies provide the statutory framework for sustainable development in the English regions, and set the context within which new-style development documents are to be drawn up at local level

▶ 'Living Places: Cleaner, Safer, Greener' provides the action plan for improving the quality of public spaces, including urban green spaces

▶ Regional Biodiversity Partnerships advise regional decision-makers on biodiversity issues

▶ The 'National Ambient Noise Strategy' for England to tackle noise from transport and industry is being developed

These strategies are regularly reviewed and updated. For instance the Government is committed to reviewing:

▶ the Air Quality Strategy in 2005, and

▶ priority species, the habitats list and targets under the Biodiversity Action Plan.

[16] Wales, Scotland and Northern Ireland have published policy objectives, targets and guidance of their own.

A key biodiversity priority for the Government is bringing 95 per cent of Sites of Special Scientific Interest (SSSIs) in England into favourable condition by 2010; only two-thirds of our SSSIs currently meet this target. A large area of SSSIs in England is common land and this is in disproportionately poor condition.

> ▶ **The Government is introducing a Commons Bill to enable common land to be managed sustainably at the local level, and to provide commons with additional protection against abuse, encroachment and unauthorised development. We intend to publish a draft Bill during summer 2005.**

SSSI in the Lake District with overgrazing visible to the right and heather stands on the left in good condition EN/photographer Peter Wakeley

A key element of the Government's Sustainable Farming and Food Strategy (SFFS) is protection of natural resources. For example, tackling diffuse water pollution from agriculture is the single biggest opportunity to improve the quality of the country's water. Following a joint Defra/HM Treasury consultation the Government is working with stakeholders to promote voluntary action focused on the needs of each catchment area, to increase awareness and measure how effective this approach is.

An important component of the SFFS is the new Environmental Stewardship Scheme launched by Defra in England. This is designed to encourage farmers to see farming in an environmentally enhancing way as a viable and rewarding way forward. It consists of:

Entry level: aimed at getting the majority of farmers to join schemes with simple, low-cost, options. These address problems such as water quality, the decline of farmland birds, butterflies and bumblebees, and the loss or damage of landscape features or archaeological sites.

Organic entry level: aims to increase the size of the organic farming sector and increase the existing biodiversity benefits of organic farming

Higher level: targeted at areas of highest value or particular need, including local habitats and species with complex management needs.

> ▶ **The Government is committed to bringing 43,000 farmers into the entry-level Environmental Stewardship Scheme during its first year of operations**

> ▶ **The Government will provide more permissive access to farmland under the new Environmental Stewardship Scheme**

> ▶ **The Higher Level Environmental Stewardship Scheme will be targeted at environmental priorities especially achieving the Government's biodiversity targets and addressing diffuse water pollution**

In 2004, Defra and the Department for Trade and Industry (DTI) published a strategy on non-food crops to promote and enhance the contribution which these crops can make to sustainable farming and to wider objectives including the protection of natural resources. Defra is funding a new National Non-Food Crops Centre as a focus for expertise for building non-food supply chains and has introduced a Bio-energy Infrastructure Scheme to stimulate the supply of biomass for energy.

➤ **The Government will continue to work on support for biofuels in transport and measures to stimulate bioenergy, including a feasibility study on the possible introduction of a renewable transport fuel obligation and follow-up to a task force set up to assist Government and industry in optimising the contribution of biomass energy to renewable energy targets**

Modernising delivery

The **planning system** provides a framework for managing development and the use of land in ways which take into account the sustainable use of our natural resources, for example by designing in from the outset measures to tackle issues such as flood risk, waste minimisation and recycling, water resource and energy efficiency. It also allows the views of those affected by proposed developments to be taken into account. The role of the planning system in delivering sustainable development is described in the section between Chapters 5 and 6.

New planning guidance on land use will help to develop a more integrated approach to the management of resources.

➤ **The Government will ensure that new arrangements for the protection of the historic environment are fully integrated with these planning processes and Environmental Stewardship Schemes**

The **Environment Agency** already helps to deliver the sustainable use of resources through regulation, provision of advice and working with partners. Its work is key to a range of policy initiatives including the EU Water Framework Directive and the system of Integrated Pollution Prevention and Control for industrial installations. It is also the main provider of flood risk management infrastructure.

A new **Integrated Agency** is also being established, bringing together English Nature, the environmental functions of the Rural Development Service and much of the Countryside Agency. The new agency will be responsible for championing the integrated management of the resource of nature, nature conservation, biodiversity, landscape, access and recreation.

➤ **The Government has introduced a Natural Environment and Rural Communities Draft Bill to Parliament for pre-legislative scrutiny to establish a new Integrated Agency. The Agency will operate within the context of sustainable development.**

Each region sets its own objectives and priorities for natural resource protection and enhancement in its regional sustainable development framework (see Chapter 7). These inform regional and sub-regional strategies. At the community level, the Environment Agency, English Nature and Countryside Agency have all shown what can be done by harnessing the energy and commitment of communities. Work that actively involves communities in protecting natural resources and enhancing their environment will be promoted through **Community Action 2020 – Together We Can**.

In the **marine environment**, we need a more integrated framework for the management and protection of our marine and coastal environment. The Government's first Marine Stewardship Report[17] adopted an ecosystem approach to turn its vision of clean, healthy, safe, productive and biologically diverse oceans and seas into reality.

Integrated Marine Management

The Review of Marine Nature Conservation was established in 1999 and collected advice from across Government, the devolved administrations and interest groups. Drawing on an Irish Sea Pilot the Review developed proposals which, when taken together, outline an ecosystem approach for the marine environment. Government's responses to the Review will need to be applied on a number of different administrative and political scales. This is a significant development in our approach to the marine environment, which will be based on greater regionalisation and increased stakeholder participation.

A pilot project in the Irish Sea is examining the practicality of Marine Spatial Planning as a tool to help implement the ecosystem approach, promote sustainable development and contribute to integrated coastal zone management. The pilot will complete around the end of the year.

> ❯ **The Government will introduce a Marine Bill in the next Parliament to improve the current framework within which those who regulate marine activities can ensure the sustainable use and protection of our marine resources. This framework will allow the different uses of the sea – including wildlife protection and human activities – to develop harmoniously.**

*Ground pollution in Thames estuary, London
Julio Etchart/Still Pictures*

4. Tackling degraded resources and environmental inequalities

As well as tackling the pressures on the environment today, we need to address the negative effects on plants and animals, air, water and soil quality as a result of human activities dating as far back as the beginning of the industrial revolution. This inheritance of degraded resources has led to social and economic deprivation, as well as a poorer environment and ill health. Improving the local environment is therefore often a starting point for wider regeneration activities.

---

[17] Defra, 2002, 'Safeguarding our Seas: a strategy for the conservation and sustainable development of our marine environment'.

Rawdon Colliery bringing derelict land into green use

Rawdon Colliery is located at Moira, Leicestershire approximately 3 miles north of Junction 11 of the M42. The site comprises a former tip, spoil heaps, railway sidings and main colliery buildings. It was transferred from British Coal to English Partnerships in December 1996 and subsequently to East Midland Development Agency in April 1999. The regeneration of Rawdon Colliery has been a unique partnership involving the reclamation and servicing of 58 hectares of land – 7 hectares for industrial development and the remainder for woodland planting and the construction of the National Forest Millennium Discovery Centre (Conkers) by the Heart of the National Forest Foundation. Reclamation by the East Midlands Development Agency through English Partnerships' National Coalfields Programme (£3.8 million) has been complemented by various funding sources. The site forms part of a semi-rural economy and the project has created additional employment by diversification into quality industrial activity, tourism and leisure.

ODPM

The Government is committed to working with a range of private and community sector partners to recover and enhance degraded resources through schemes such as Newlands.

Tackling inherited degradation – Newlands

Newlands is a £23 million scheme developed by the Northwest Development Agency and the Forestry Commission to reclaim large areas of derelict, underused and neglected land across Northwest England. It will take an integrated and innovative approach to create community woodlands that provide recreational areas, benefits for business, a boost to healthy living and a significant increase in woodland cover. This will be delivered through a range of private and voluntary partners. The first five-year phase of the scheme will target areas in the Mersey Belt aiming to recover 435 hectares of brownfield land. Phase two will extend across the region to include Cumbria, Lancashire and the rest of Cheshire.

Globally and within the UK, deprived and excluded communities are affected disproportionately by degraded natural resources and their associated risks. Minimum standards for a decent and healthy environment are set by adopting and enforcing the international, European and national policy and regulatory frameworks. People will be able to see what they can expect from their environment and who is responsible for ensuring it is of a high quality. They can also help report failures to meet these standards.

> ▶ **The Government will bring this information together in an integrated framework and publish details of this at www.sustainable-development.gov.uk**

In the UK, environmental degradation is a real problem for many of the most deprived communities. This is both because of the historic legacy mentioned above and because of difficulties in finding effective ways for agencies and communities to identify priorities and work together to tackle them. In addition, it is important to ensure there are sufficient disincentives for environmental pollution.

> **The Government will collaborate with the Environment Agency and others to look at proposals to develop a scheme of civil penalties for certain environmental offences to ensure that we have more effective means of tackling environmental pollution and environmental inequalities**

More on how we propose to tackle inequalities at local level is set out in Chapter 6.

Tackling environmental inequalities not only requires the protection and enhancement of natural resources in the most environmentally-deprived areas but also work to improve wider access, and to provide social benefits such as better health. The Countryside and Rights of Way Act (2000) gives people new rights to walk in areas of open country and registered common land. However before the new right comes into effect the land must be mapped so everyone knows where they can walk.

> **All access land in England will be mapped by 2006**

> **The Government will take further measures to achieve our aim that everyone should have good opportunities to enjoy the natural environment. Action to improve access to coastal land will be our first priority**

Friends of Phoenix Park, Wolverhampton

There are important links between access to a safe, clean and attractive environment and the ability of individuals to lead healthy, active lifestyles. For example, British Trust for Conservation Volunteers was selected in this year's ODPM Special Grants Programme (2005/06) bidding round to receive funding for their strategic work programme supporting 'green' gym training programmes, promoting health and partnership working.

To realise the full recreational and health benefits that should arise from better access, the Countryside Agency is carrying out a Diversity Review to investigate how we can improve opportunities for a broader cross-section of society to enjoy the countryside.

> **A diversity action plan will follow from the Review, and will be put in place in 2005/06**

The Government wants all children and young people to see and understand the world around them too, from their own school grounds to the many and varied landscapes of the UK and beyond. We will work with schools and providers of educational experiences outside the classroom to launch a 'Manifesto for education outside the classroom' to set out what opportunities parents and young people can expect.

Our landscapes and seascapes are inseparable from our culture, bearing the imprints of generations of land use. Our physical and mental health is reliant on the quality of the environment. There must also be access to a variety of well-managed and maintained green spaces for leisure, sport, recreation and general public benefit to help people choose healthy lifestyles, in urban as well as rural areas. Physical inactivity has serious effects on human health, which according to recent research costs the UK economy more than £8 billion a year.[18]

> ❯ **Defra and the Department of Health will enter into a Strategic Partnership Agreement in 2005 to help realise the shared benefit of an enhanced environment to improving health**

> ❯ **The Government will report on progress in pursuing its Children's Health and Environment Action Plan by 2007**

> ❯ **As part of Community Action 2020 – Together We Can we will promote ways to help communities improve their environment and participate in plans which shape their area's future**

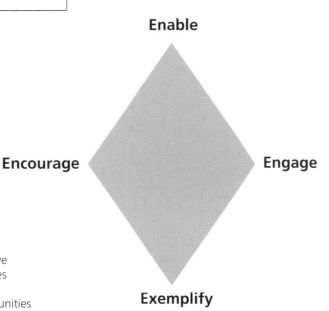

Our integrated approach to protecting natural resources and enhancing the environment

- Developing the evidence base on environmental limits
- Web based material on the UK's environmental framework
- Marine Bill
- Commons Bill
- Strong capacity building from the new integrated agency and the Environment Agency
- Global Environmental Facility Funding

Enable

Encourage

- Environmental Stewardship
- Regulatory framework
- Water Framework Directive
- Further CAP reform
- Further CFP reform
- Darwin Initiative
- Flagship Species Fund
- Global Opportunities Fund
- Civil penalties options for the Environment Agency

Engage

- Community engagement to provide better access to the countryside
- Local Biodiversity Action Plans
- Stakeholder events to develop a natural resources vision
- The Diversity Action Plan

Exemplify

- Environmental issues integrated in poverty reduction strategies
- Integrated policy approach
- Strong strategic partnership between DH and Defra to link health and environmental outcomes

---

[18] Dr William Bird, RSPB and Faculty of Public Health, 2004, 'Natural Fit – can biodiversity and greenspace increase levels of physical activity?'.

5. Measuring our progress

There are many ways to measure how we protect our natural resources and our progress in environmental enhancement. Internationally we are supporting work to develop indicators for global biodiversity under the Convention on Biological Diversity, and are researching indicators on environment and health.

We will be making revisions in due course to our sustainable development indicators for river quality to take account of the environmental objectives which will be set for water bodies under the Water Framework Directive.

Indicators to be used to report progress will include all indicators within the UK Framework set that are relevant to natural resources and in addition other indicators relevant to the priorities of the UK Government Strategy:

- ❯ **Bird populations*:** bird population indices (a) farmland birds* (b) woodland birds* (c) birds of coasts and estuaries* (d) wintering wetland birds
- ❯ **Biodiversity conservation:** (a) priority species status (b) priority habitat status
- ❯ **Farming and environmental stewardship:** *(to be developed to monitor progress in new stewardship schemes)*
- ❯ **Agriculture sector:** fertiliser input, farmland bird populations and ammonia and methane emissions and output
- ❯ **Land use:** area used for agriculture, woodland, water or river, urban (contextual indicator)
- ❯ **Land recycling:** (a) new dwellings built on previously developed land or through conversions (b) all new development on previously developed land
- ❯ **Environmental equality*:** *(measures to be developed)*
- ❯ **Dwelling density:** average density of new housing
- ❯ **Households and dwellings:** households, single person households and dwelling stock (contextual indicator)
- ❯ **Fish stocks*:** fish stocks around the UK within sustainable limits
- ❯ **Ecological impacts of air pollution*:** area of UK habitat sensitive to acidification and eutrophication with critical load exceedences
- ❯ **Emissions of air pollutants:** SO_2, NO_x, NH_3 and PM_{10} emissions and GDP
- ❯ **River quality*:** rivers of good (a) biological (b) chemical quality
- ❯ **Water stress:** *(to be developed to monitor the impacts of water shortages)*
- ❯ **Flooding:** *(to be developed to monitor sustainable approaches to ongoing flood management)*

Note some indicators are relevant to other parts of the Strategy and are also listed in other chapters.

* Indicator is included in the UK Framework Indicators

Planning – with sustainable development at its heart

The planning system is key to achieving sustainable development. The Government's new planning policy statement 'Delivering Sustainable Development' (PPS 1) sets out our vision for planning in England and the key policies which will underpin it. PPS1 makes clear that sustainable development is at the heart of the planning system. It sets the framework for reflecting the duty in the Planning and Compulsory Purchase Act 2004 for regional and local plans to be prepared with a view to contributing to sustainable development.

Other planning policies, set out in the Government's Planning Policy Statements and Planning Policy Guidance notes, complement PPS1 in delivering sustainable development:

> Planning policies for housing ensure that brownfield land is developed first for new housing, and that new housing is built at higher densities than previously, reducing the need for development on greenfield sites

> Other national policies ensure that new developments are located in areas such as town centres which are accessible by means of walking, cycling and public transport thereby reducing reliance on the private car

> Policies for the natural and historic environment ensure the conservation and reuse of buildings and the protection of wildlife resources, and

> Policies for rural areas ensure that there are strict controls on development in the open countryside and that our finest countryside and landscapes are protected for the benefit of everyone.

The Government will also revise its policy on "planning obligations" in Spring 2005, to make it clearer how developers can be required through the planning system to take certain actions in order to ensure development is acceptable and in line with sustainable communities policies. For example, the revised policy will set out how planning obligations may be used to require a developer to provide a contribution towards affordable housing or to compensate for loss of habitat or damage to the environment.

Sustainable development is built into every stage of the planning process. Regional plans, called Regional Spatial Strategies (RSS), are drawn up by Regional Assemblies (the regional planning body). The RSS, incorporating a Regional Transport Strategy (RTS), provides a spatial framework to inform the preparation of Local Development Documents (LDDs). These documents form the portfolio which collectively delivers the spatial planning strategy for a local planning authority's area. The RSS also informs the preparation of Local Transport Plans (LTPs), and regional and sub-regional strategies and programmes that have a bearing on the use of land.

The RSS should articulate a vision for the region for a 15-20 year period and show how this will contribute to achieving sustainable development objectives. Both RSSs and LDDs should be developed in partnership with a wide range of stakeholders, with appropriate community involvement at all stages.

RSSs should contain spatial policies for:

➤ the scale and distribution of provision for new housing

➤ priorities for the environment, such as countryside and biodiversity protection, and

➤ transport, infrastructure, economic development, agriculture, minerals extraction and waste treatment and disposal.

As an integral part of reviewing and updating the RSS and LDDs, planning authorities are required to undertake a Sustainability Appraisal (SA). Following consultation in 2004, the Government will publish final guidance for these appraisals in 2005. In advance of this guidance, the Government will issue interim advice on the key SA topics raised during and since the consultation. Good practice examples of SAs will be published on the ODPM website.

SAs will comply fully with the European Directive on Strategic Environmental Assessment.

New Homes being built in the Thames Gateway

Chapter 6
From Local to Global: Creating Sustainable Communities and a Fairer World

The facts

> 79% of people in the least deprived areas in the UK enjoy where they live compared with 46% in the most deprived areas. Those living in deprived areas are also the least likely to participate in community activities[1]

> The gap in male life expectancy at birth between Manchester and East Dorset is nearly eight and a half years[2]

> Over a quarter of children and a fifth of pensioners in the UK are living in relative poverty (after housing costs)[3]

> Average life expectancy at birth in the UK is currently 78 years whilst the global average is 65 years[4]

> An estimated 114 million children of primary age in the world are not enrolled in school, depriving one in very five children of access to even the most basic education[5]

> Over 800 million adults are illiterate in the world, 90 per cent of which live in developing countries[6]

> More than 800 million people go to bed hungry every day...300 million are children. Of these 300 million children, only eight percent are victims of famine or other emergency situations: more than 90 percent are suffering long-term malnourishment and micronutrient deficiency[7]

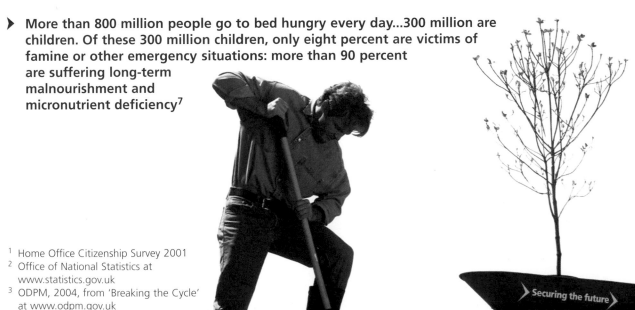

Securing the future

[1] Home Office Citizenship Survey 2001
[2] Office of National Statistics at www.statistics.gov.uk
[3] ODPM, 2004, from 'Breaking the Cycle' at www.odpm.gov.uk
[4] WHO at www.who.int/en/
[5] UN at www.un.org/
[6] UNESCO figures in 2005 report at www.unesco.org
[7] UN

Summary

Creating sustainable communities everywhere is a challenging task. It requires us to integrate the delivery of social, economic and environmental goals, to take a co-ordinated approach to delivering public services that work for everyone, including the most disadvantaged, and to think strategically for the long-term.

Taking it on consultation responses

A key message from the 'Taking it on' consultation was that the public sector needs to work together better in tackling issues of social and environmental justice and use existing structures to provide local services, planning and regeneration.

Consultees indicated that mixed messages from national government, for example on 'sustainable communities', 'sustainable development', 'wellbeing' and 'sustainability' can make delivery of sustainable development very difficult at the local level.

It was suggested that more leadership, awareness and understanding of sustainable development is required at the local level and that leadership on sustainable development is not visible at the national level.

Community Strategies and Local Strategic Partnerships have a key role to play in delivering sustainable development particularly in relation to housing, regeneration, transport, waste, local food, flooding, local business partnerships, and public health. But they could be used better.

Local Agenda 21 was seen as a positive initiative but respondents expressed frustration that it had been either 'lost' or 'diluted' by new processes.

Respondents felt that setting a good example was important in the promotion and delivery of sustainable development internationally. That should be demonstrated by sharing knowledge and best practice, and by applying or reforming key international agreements. The use of international aid to promote sustainable development was strongly favoured.

1. Our Approach

In this chapter we show how from the local to global level, the Government will work to create sustainable communities. The desired outcomes will vary in different places. But in all cases we aim to give people more control over decisions that affect them, focus on delivering solutions to locally identified problems, and work in partnership to tackle social, economic and environmental issues.

"Creating Sustainable Communities means putting sustainable development into practice. Sustainable Communities must combine social inclusion, homes, jobs, services, infrastructure and respect for the environment to create places where people will want to live and work now and in the future."

Rt. Hon. John Prescott MP,
Deputy Prime Minister, February 2005

➤ At the local level, the strategy sets out how the Government's Sustainable Communities agenda will improve people's lives by delivering better neighbourhoods; cleaner, safer, greener, healthier communities; homes for all; stronger neighbourhood engagement; and will catalyse action on sustainable development in both urban and rural areas in England. This strategy also sets out how we will deliver this through working with local government, enhanced by the work to support local leadership and skills as set out in Chapter 7

➤ At the national level, we must provide opportunities for everyone to fulfil their potential. We must ensure that Government policy improve the life chances of the most vulnerable groups in society

➤ At the global level, the key issue is how to meet the Millennium Development Goals (MDGs). The strategy looks at how we will apply the principles of good governance and partnership, working on locally identified priorities, to be able to tackle social, economic and environmental inequalities

2. At the local level in England: Sustainable Communities

The drive to improve neighbourhood participation, address inequalities and support delivery at the local level is at the heart of the Sustainable Communities agenda.

> ❯ Our aim is to create sustainable communities in England that embody the principles of sustainable development at the local level:[8]
>
>   ❯ balancing and integrating the social, economic and environmental components of their community
>
>   ❯ meeting the needs of existing and future generations, and
>
>   ❯ respecting the needs of other communities in the wider region or internationally to make their communities sustainable.
>
> Sustainable communities are places where people want to live and work, now and in the future. They meet the diverse needs of existing and future residents, are sensitive to their environment, and contribute to a high quality of life. They are safe and inclusive, well planned, built and run, and offer equality of opportunity and good services for all.
>
> Sustainable communities should be:
>
> ❯ **ACTIVE, INCLUSIVE AND SAFE** – fair, tolerant and cohesive with a strong local culture and other shared community activities
>
> ❯ **WELL RUN** – with effective and inclusive participation, representation and leadership
>
> ❯ **ENVIRONMENTALLY SENSITIVE** – providing places for people to live that are considerate of the environment
>
> ❯ **WELL DESIGNED AND BUILT** – featuring a quality built and natural environment
>
> ❯ **WELL CONNECTED** – with good transport services and communication linking people to jobs, schools, health and other services
>
> ❯ **THRIVING** – with a flourishing and diverse local economy
>
> ❯ **WELL SERVED** – with public, private, community and voluntary services that are appropriate to people's needs and accessible to all
>
> ❯ **FAIR FOR EVERYONE** – including those in other communities, now and in the future
>
> * For a comprehensive statement of the Government's view of what makes a sustainable community, see Annex A

Better neighbourhoods

People's local neighbourhoods matter to them and have a significant impact on their quality of life – whether they live, work or play there. People want to be able to have a say in, and make a more tangible contribution to, the way their local area and services are managed.

We aim to make local services work together to ensure we have cleaner, safer, greener and healthier neighbourhoods for everyone, where local people have their say.

[8] ODPM, 2005, 'Sustainable Communities: People, Places and Prosperity' and 'Sustainable Communities: Homes for All' at www.odpm.gov.uk/fiveyearstrategy

Achievements since 1999

Places are **getting cleaner:**

> the national survey of local environmental quality (LEQSE) started three years ago has shown that the percentage of areas with unacceptable standards of cleanliness has fallen eight per cent in two years

> the introduction of Best Value Performance Indicators around litter and detritus are already delivering improvements in service management and focussing action on problem areas, and

> we have worked with local authorities and others to strengthen legislation and provide the right powers and responsibilities, in particular through the Local Government Act 2003, Anti-Social Behaviour Act 2003 and proposals in the Clean Neighbourhoods and Environment Bill.

Places are **getting safer:**

> British Crime Survey shows crime is down 30 per cent since 1997 and concern about anti-social behaviour after rising through the 1990s has fallen five per cent since 2002/03, following more concerted action and new improved tools like Anti-Social Behaviour Orders, and

> neighbourhood wardens reassure people about their community. The 500 neighbourhood warden schemes, with over 3000 wardens have delivered a 28 per cent fall in crime in comparison to other areas. Proposals for neighbourhood policing and 25 000 community support officers will build on this foundation.

Places are **getting more attractive:**

> we have seen a renaissance in our major cities and reversed the outflow of people and investment, backed by massive improvements in the public realm and quality of design, vitality and vibrancy and investment and public programmes to rebuild our schools, hospitals and infrastructure for the 21st century

> our £200 million programme to support more action on managing the quality of local environments has seen a doubling since 2002 of the parks and green spaces awarded the Green Flag Award in recognition of their standard of management and maintenance. Public satisfaction with parks and open spaces has increased from 62.5 per cent to 71 per cent in the last three years, and

> the £6 million Home Office/Neighbourhood Renewal Unit Community Cohesion Pathfinder programme (2001-2004) has developed a range of approaches to building cohesion in neighbourhoods.

The Government's priorities are to:

> create attractive and welcoming parks, play areas and public spaces

> engage and empower local people and communities

> improve the physical infrastructure of places

> make places cleaner and maintain them better

> make places safer and tackle anti-social behaviour

> improve health by encouraging and supporting healthy lifestyles, and

> tackle inequalities and support the needs of children and young people.

The Government has set a new target to deliver cleaner, safer, greener public spaces and to improve the quality of the built environment in deprived areas and across the country with measurable improvement by 2008.

Our strategy to deliver cleaner, safer, greener and healthier communities is being delivered through a cross-government programme supporting practitioners at all levels.

At the heart of the programme is support for local authorities to raise standards. People expect local authorities to maintain the quality of their local environments – they expect less litter, graffiti, fly-posting and dog-fouling, and fewer abandoned vehicles. Local authorities will receive around £7 billion for local environmental services over the next three years and £3 billion for highway maintenance and street lighting. On top of this, specific programmes to deliver decent homes, neighbourhood renewal, housing market renewal and new housing growth will include contributions to improving the local environment. Local authorities, in their leadership role, can also influence the resources and actions of other public bodies, business, charitable bodies, and voluntary and community organisations, which is estimated at £8 billion a year in total, to achieve a shared vision for transforming local environments.

The Government will also provide extra powers to deal with anti-social behaviour, in particular on low level disorder and environmental offences which can degrade the local environment through the Clean Neighbourhoods and Environment Bill. We will incentivise local authorities to take effective action to improve their local environment, by giving this the weight it deserves in the measurement and assessment of local authority performance in this area.

The Cleaner, Safer, Greener Communities programme will engage local people in decisions about the services they get, empower them to trigger action and make service providers responsive to their needs, and give them opportunities to drive improvement through neighbourhood arrangements. The programme will work closely with our Neighbourhood Renewal programmes to focus action in deprived areas, by supporting the delivery of our new floor target to narrow the gap between the worst off areas and people and the rest.

The challenge for local authorities and others is to spend the resources already available by joining up service delivery and working better in partnership with other public bodies, local business and people. We will support this through streamlining ODPM and Home Office funding streams into a single 'Safer and Stronger Communities Fund' worth £660m over the next three years. This fund will be used to reduce crime and fear of crime, improve public spaces, build the capacity of local communities to influence the decision making and delivery of services and improve the quality of life for people living in deprived areas. The fund is being rolled out to local authorities in England and will form the basis of one of the three blocks of new Local Area Agreements (LAAs).

> **The Government will commit £5 million over the next three years to establish a 'How To' programme that works with and for practitioners to provide guidance, action learning and peer support on improving the liveability of town centres, residential areas and streets and parks and open spaces**

Children planting trees to support the National Forest project
Source: National Forest Company

Work in addition to this programme includes:

> **CABE Space**, the national champion for parks and public spaces, will work with central and local government and other organisations concerned with public spaces to advise on high quality planning, design, management and maintenance

> An expanded **Green Flag Award** scheme will help recognise and reward progress in well-maintained and managed green spaces[9]

> **Sustainable transport measures** will allow people to see alternatives to the car as attractive and viable choices. Measures include walking and cycling action plans, school and green travel plans[10], and publicity and information provision on public transport services. For example school travel plans encourage schools and local authorities to work together to promote walking, cycling, public transport and car share schemes. It is intended that travel plans be introduced into every school in England by 2010. Collectively sustainable transport measures aim to reduce air pollution and congestion, improve access to services, increase physical activity and improve safety for pedestrians and cyclists

> **Measures to champion the use of public space to ensure healthy lifestyles** such as 'Walking your way to health' and Community Forests will be promoted

> **'Extended Schools'** will work in partnership with local agencies to provide a range of local services including, for example, NHS Stop Smoking sessions and sexual health services. The schools are particularly important for rural areas and areas of disadvantage, where they offer a first point of contact for children and families, and

> The **School Fruit and Vegetable Scheme** is part of the '5 A DAY' programme to increase fruit and vegetable consumption. Under the Scheme, all four to six year old children in LEA maintained infant, primary and special schools will be entitled to a free piece of fruit or vegetable each school day.

Communities are also being encouraged to improve community safety, health and the local environment through:

> Community Action 2020: Together We Can

> the activities of Groundwork and other development trusts

> the Living Spaces scheme

---

[9] See www.greenflagaward.org.uk
[10] DfES and DfT, 2003, 'Travelling to school: an action plan'

> cultural regeneration programmes

> 'Home Zones' – shared road space initiatives

> neighbourhood policing

> the 'Communities for Health' programme, and

> the 'Together' action plan to tackle anti-social behaviour.

Photo source: 3rd Avenue

In 2003, the Government launched the Sustainable Travel Town project. Over the next five years, the Government is making available £10 million to work with Darlington, Peterborough and Worcester to introduce an intensive, comprehensive and strategic package to promote safe and pleasant walking, cycling and bus use for all kinds of trips across the towns. The aim is to create three sustainable travel demonstration towns to act as models for other local authorities and show what can be achieved through a combined package of measures to increase travel choices.

Homes for All

A decent, affordable home is a key requirement of a sustainable community. The Government aims to meet this basic need. But it is important that we do so in a way which respects the principles of sustainable development, creating homes in communities with the infrastructure, jobs and services needed to support them, and being sensitive to the needs of the environment.

The scale of the challenge is clear: the total number of households in England is expected to increase by nearly 190 000 per year to 2021. Many of them will be single-person households, reflecting wider trends in society such as changing family relationships, longer lives and greater personal wealth. Yet since the 1960s we have failed as a country to build enough homes to meet these needs, which has meant that a decent home has become less affordable for many people.

Any responsible government must plan to address this challenge. The Government's five year plan, 'Sustainable Communities: Homes for All'[11], sets out how the Government is working to increase the supply of new homes in a responsible way, by:

> **Making best use of land:** Since 1997 the Government has already increased the proportion of housing development on brownfield land from 56 per cent to 67 per cent, and raised the densities of new development from 25 dwellings per hectare to 33 dwellings per hectare. This means that the proposed 1.1 million new homes in the wider South East by 2016 can be delivered using 3300 hectares less greenfield land than previous plans for 900 000 homes would have required at 1997 density rates – saving an area the size of Oxford. The Government will go further: we have extended the Density Direction – which enables the Secretary of State to call in proposals for low density developments – to other areas of high housing demand in the South West and East of England. We will be consulting on a new Green Belt Direction to strengthen protection of the green belt. New planning guidance[12] sets out a framework within which former industrial land can be treated and safely brought back into new uses, including housing, in support of the "brownfield first" objective

[11] ODPM, 2005, 'Sustainable Communities: Homes for All' at
www.odpm.gov.uk/odpm/fiveyearstrategy/homes_for_all.htm
[12] ODPM, 2004, 'Planning policy statement 23' at www.odpm.gov.uk

> **Proper management of flood risk:** In line with national planning policy guidance there will be flood risk assessments for publicly funded developments in the Thames Gateway and new flood defence schemes; and integrated water management studies at Ashford, supported by a new working relationship with the Environment Agency as our key advisors

> **Investing in infrastructure:** Where new homes are needed, the Government is investing to ensure that they are supported by the transport, schools and hospitals needed to ensure communities are viable in the long-term – for example £3.1 billion for new transport schemes in four Growth Areas in the wider South East

> **Promoting high standards of construction and design:** The Government will demonstrate a new Code for Sustainable Buildings in a range of locations, including the Thames Gateway, aimed at delivering significant resource efficiency savings. We will continue to raise standards for the energy efficiency of new homes. By 2010 we aim to improve the average energy efficiency of the domestic housing stock by 20% compared with 2000 (Chapter 4 describes this work in more detail).

Elsewhere, the challenge is to revive communities in decline. The Government is investing £1.2 billion through its Market Renewal programme to tackle low housing demand in parts of the North and Midlands, through holistic regeneration programmes which may involve some demolition. In recognition of the environmental and social benefits of avoiding unnecessary demolition, the Sustainable Development Commission (SDC) and ODPM are looking at opportunities to improve and remodel existing housing in areas of low demand. By the same token in the growth areas, the SDC will look at the opportunities to improve and regenerate existing low density communities to reduce the pressure on land and resources. And in rural areas, the Government has enabled local authorities to use the planning system to allocate sites just for affordable housing to meet the needs of key workers and local people on a permanent basis.

Delivering change – through community engagement

Two initiatives are working alongside one another to encourage local people to become more engaged in the communities in which they live, work, and play.

As described in Chapter 2, a cross government action plan, **'Together We Can'** is being developed to increase citizens' and communities' engagement in solving public problems and improving their quality of life.

And as part of the development of **'local:vision'** – the ten year strategy for the future of local government – the Government has set out proposals to offer new opportunities for people in all neighbourhoods to help shape the public services that they receive and become more involved in the democratic life of their communities. The Government wants to ensure that all neighbourhoods have the chance to have their say – without imposing a one-size-fits-all model – and that arrangements work through councils and local councillors.

Council staff on a walkabout with schoolchildren, surveying their local environment and listing problems in Newham
Source: 3rd Avenue

'Citizen Engagement and Public Services: Why Neighbourhoods Matter'[13] proposes developing a national framework with local government and others which sets out principles for neighbouhood arrangements. The framework will be underpinned by a 'Neighbourhoods Charter' setting out what local people should expect, both in terms of outcomes – for example, safe, clean streets – and in terms of control or influence over their neighbourhoods. The Charter could be accompanied by a menu of options from which neighbourhoods would choose – including triggers for action in response to failure or under-performance of services. The Charter would also encourage all councils to establish small funds for councillors to spend at their discretion to improve their areas in ways suggested by neighbouhood bodies.

Together, these proposals will build on work already being done at neighbourhood level, so increasing the involvement of local people and communities in the decisions that affect them, and strengthening and reinvigorating local democracy.

We recognise that if people are to take up the opportunities for involvement, it is important to invest in building their skills, abilities, knowledge and confidence, as well as expanding learning and development within the public services, so that professionals, practitioners and policy-makers are better equipped to engage with citizens and communities. 'Firm Foundations' (Home Office, 2004) sets out the Government's framework for community capacity building, and identifies priorities for action, which are reflected in the Community Action 2020 – Together We Can proposals and other aspects of this strategy.

Community engagement should be central to the process of drawing up the local statutory strategic plans for the area, such as the local development documents, including area actions plans in the **Local Development Framework (LDF), the Sustainable Community Strategy**, and the **Local Area Agreement (LAA)** as well as to solving public problems. Community buy-in is essential in achieving local ownership of and legitimacy for these plans, which will shape the long-term vision and the future distribution of land and development in an authority's area. Local action-planning, for example by voluntary groups, in the shape of parish plans, neighbourhood action plans, and other forms of participative involvement, offers an effective way of engaging local citizens and communities in contributing to those processes.

Local planning authorities will set out in their Statement of Community Involvement (SCI) how communities will be engaged in the preparation and revision of LDFs, and consulted on planning applications. SCIs will also be linked to the broader Community Action 2020 – Together We Can programme.

Sustainable Community Strategies which are key to delivering the vision for sustainable communities set out at the start of the chapter, will be drawn up by the local authority and the Local Strategic Partnership (LSP), in consultation with the community[14]. These will evolve from Community Strategies to give a greater emphasis to sustainable development objectives which are necessary for creating an area where people genuinely want to live long-term.

[13] ODPM and HO, 2005, 'Citizen Engagement and Public Services: Why Neighbourhoods Matter' at www.odpm.gov.uk
[14] OPDM, 2005, 'Government Vibrant Leadership'.

> **The Government will consider with our partners how to revise the existing guidance and develop toolkits and other materials to support local authorities and LSPs when reviewing and preparing their Sustainable Community Strategies**

> **As part of Community Action 2020 – Together We Can, the Government will celebrate successful Sustainable Community Strategies, parish plans and neighbourhood plans, looking particularly for those that do most to build on Local Agenda 21, are innovative in their approach and help achieve a step change in sustainable development**

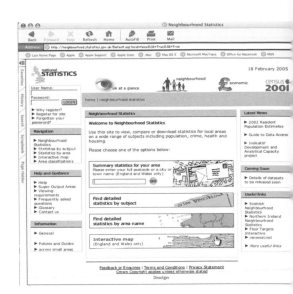

Neighbourhood Statistics website

To encourage the preparation of parish plans which cover social, economic and environmental goals in rural communities, the Government will provide practical support on sustainable development and will build the capacity of those involved in supporting communities to cover the full range of sustainable development issues. In 'Firm Foundations' the Government has also identified the need to develop good practice guidelines to support local action planning in general and how it can contribute to sustainable development.

Delivering the local vision of sustainable communities as set out in these documents, needs a joined-up approach at the local level, with strong local leadership by the local authority. The Government, in developing **local:vision**, has set out a vision of strong, self confident local authorities, working closely with their local partners, to lead actively the development of sustainable communities and engaging their citizens[15].

Public access to better local information is vital if communities are going to engage with local service providers.

> **The Government is committed to ensuring that people have this access in order to contribute effectively to decision-making and to increasing the transparency of Government and other public authorities. People can gain access to information held by public authorities under the Freedom of Information Act[16] and Environmental Information Regulations[17].**

Services like neighbourhood statistics[18] and the Environment Agency's 'what's in your backyard'[19] already provide anyone with detailed local information about how their neighbourhood compares with other areas on many key issues. Other websites set out how well local service providers are meeting the needs of their communities. For example the website www.auditcommission.gov.uk/cpa shows how well your local council meets the needs of your area, including a very broad set of shared priorities linked to the goals of sustainable communities. Armed with this information, anyone can gain a better understanding of what the key priorities for an area are likely to be.

---

15 ODPM, 2004, 'The future of local government: developing a ten year vision'.
16 The Freedom of Information Act 2000.
17 Environmental Information Regulations 2004 on public access to environmental information aim to ensure that all decisions to release or withhold environmental information are made in the public interest and that public utilities, waste contractors, airports, and other businesses proactively disseminate environmental information and respond appropriately to requests.
18 www.neighbourhood.statistics.gov.uk
19 www.environment-agency.gov.uk

However, there is a lack of consistent comparable data about the local environment so the Government makes this commitment to:

> **Provide better joined-up public information at a local level both in the form of statistics and through easy to understand mapping services. This will include providing over the next five years a consistent and comparable picture of the local environment at the neighbourhood level as part of the neighbourhood statistics website, and improving access to information about the environment by promoting websites such as 'what's in your backyard' and noisemapping.org**

> **Work with the Environment Agency, local authorities and others to produce and maintain a single electronic portal to environmental registers of environmental information in 2005**

The commitments above also support the implementation of the Aarhus Convention which will strengthen public access to environmental information and public involvement in environmental decision-making, to which the Government is fully committed. The UK has recently ratified the Aarhus Convention as a sign of this commitment.

Delivering change – central and local government working together

Central and local government have already agreed seven 'Shared Priorities' where local government will make a real difference to local communities and help deliver on the Government's national priorities. These Shared Priorities are:

> Creating safer and stronger communities

> Improving the quality of life of older people and children, young people and families at risk

> Meeting transport needs more effectively

> Promoting healthier communities and narrowing health inequalities

> Promoting the economic vitality of localities

> Raising standards across our schools, and

> Transforming the local environment.

Photo source: 3rd Avenue

> **The Government will publish a new guide to delivering the Shared Priorities in 2005 which will set out the distinctive outcomes for each Priority linked to sustainable development**

Performance on how well the Shared Priorities are being delivered locally will be measured through the Comprehensive Performance Assessment for all local authorities. To complement this:

> **The Audit Commission will launch a revised set of voluntary Local Quality of Life Indicators in 2005 which can help monitor local progress in delivering sustainable communities. The publication will also include information on other indicators such as ecological footprinting and links to tools.**

These indicators will help LSPs and others at the local level to link their priorities to wider regional and international goals and will also complement the Area Profiles of all local authorities being developed by the Audit Commission.

To give local authorities and their LSPs greater freedom to explore local solutions to local problems, Local Area Agreements (LAAs) are being piloted in 21 areas with a further phase of 40 agreements to be in place by April 2006. LAAs will benefit from less ring-fenced funding, less red tape and more flexibility in how they work. Authorities and their partners will negotiate shared key outcomes with government offices, reflecting locally and nationally agreed priorities. LSPs will co-ordinate the contribution of the local partners, including the community and voluntary sector to ensure their full engagement. We are encouraging pilot local areas to be ambitious in thinking about their proposed outcomes and the partnerships that will support them.

LAAs could be vehicles through which many of the initiatives outlined in this chapter – such as those on health, inequalities, transport and employment – could be addressed in a joined-up way at the local level. Some areas, where there are pathfinder projects investigating improved co-ordination of rural delivery at the local level, have also been chosen as pilots for Local Area Agreements. We are keen to explore the links between the two initiatives, and the selection of Dorset as both LAA pilot and pathfinder will, in particular, provide an opportunity to do this.

LAAs will pool a number of funding streams from central government departments. LAAs are structured around three key themes – Children and Young People; Safer and Stronger Communities; and Healthier Communities and Older People. They will offer real opportunities for local authorities and their partners to work together to agree priorities and to respond flexibly to improve outcomes, including promoting sustainable development.

Tackling local inequalities

This Government has a clear vision that within 10-20 years no-one should be seriously disadvantaged because of where they live.[20] The approaches set out above will create sustainable communities in many places, but some neighbourhoods will need more help.

---

[20] ODPM, 2005, 'Making it happen in neighbourhoods', at www.neighbourhood.gov.uk

Achievements in tackling inequalities since 1999

▶ Over £1.6 billion invested since 1997 in neighbourhood renewal for the most deprived areas in the country, with the New Deal for Communities improving how people feel about their area and the National Strategy for Neighbourhood Renewal helping to narrow the gap between deprived areas and the rest on key education, crime, and worklessness indicators.

▶ There has been a joined-up approach to community cohesion, to ensure it is embedded at an early stage into the regeneration process[21].

▶ Child poverty has declined since 1997. In 2002/03 there were 700 000 fewer children living in relative poverty than in 1996/97. It is estimated that by 2004/05, if the Government had taken no action 1.5 million more children would be in poverty.

▶ Educational attainment has risen at all levels, especially in primary schools. At key stage 2 (11 year olds) the proportion of pupils achieving the expected level in English rose from 63 per cent in 1997 to 77 per cent in 2004. The proportion of pupils achieving the expected level in Maths rose from 62 per cent to 74 per cent over the same period.

▶ There has been a fall in the teenage pregnancy rate. Conception rates among girls under 18 fell by 9.4 per cent between 1998 and 2002.

▶ The number of people in work has increased since 1997. In 2004, there were 1.85 million more people in work than there were in 1997. There have been faster than average increases in employment among disadvantaged groups like lone parents, people with disabilities and those over 50 years old.

▶ Pensioner poverty has declined. Since 1997 the number of pensioners living in relative low income has fallen by 500 000. The number of pensioners living in absolute poverty has fallen by 1.8 million.

▶ There has been a significant decline in the number of people sleeping rough. The number of rough sleepers has fallen by over 70 per cent since 1998.

The recent joint report between the Prime Minister's Strategy Unit[22] and ODPM set out the case for Government continuing to take action in poor areas. The Government acknowledges that there is still much to do – and together with regional agencies, and local and neighbourhood partners, it will continue to improve life for those living in the poorest areas in England.

In taking forward our work to tackle deprived places the Government will:

▶ **Continue to provide extra support to LSPs in the most disadvantaged areas through the Neighbourhood Renewal Fund and to focus on raising standards in mainstream public services in all deprived communities**

▶ **Encourage businesses to work through the LSPs to help identify business opportunities in deprived areas and to support development of their workforce**

---

[21] HO and ODPM, 2003, 'Community Cohesion Advice for those designing, developing and delivering Area Based Initiatives' and HO and ODPM, 2004, 'Building Cohesion into Area Based Initiatives', at www.homeoffice.gov.uk
[22] PMSU and ODPM, 2005, 'Improving the prospects of people living in areas of multiple deprivation in England'.

> **From 2006, provide through the Safer and Stronger Communities Fund will provide core funding to Community Empowerment Networks to co-ordinate, on behalf of all partners, the LSP's community empowerment activities. These networks will have access to Community Action 2020 – Together We Can mentors**

> **Ensure that appraisal of policy proposals takes account of their local and distributional impact to avoid adverse impacts on the most deprived areas and social groups**

> **Continue to set "floor targets" as part of Public Spending Agreements (PSA) in Spending Reviews. These ensure that Government performance is measured on how well we are closing the gap between the most deprived areas and social groups, and the rest of the country.[23] Refined floor targets, effective from April 2005, have a new target on liveability**

There is evidence from several studies (mainly North American) that the less affluent have better health and better quality of life outcomes when they share neighbourhoods with more affluent, better educated, individuals.[24]

While planning legislation now requires that new housing developments contain a mix of types of tenure and values of properties, poverty remains concentrated at neighbourhood level: between 10 and 30 per cent of Income Support and Jobseekers' Allowance claimants live in the five per cent most income-deprived wards. Some of these neighbourhoods have always been deprived but there has also been growth in economic segregation since the 1970s focused on areas with social housing.

Differences in health and other life outcomes for different social classes could be further decreased by tackling this "economic segregation".

The Government will explore the effects of policies to reduce economic segregation in more depth, with initial activity focused on:

> **UK research using existing data sources on current associations between economic segregation and health and other outcomes**

> **Development of sensitive indicators of economic segregation**

> **Assessing the positive (and any negative) impacts of breaking up carefully selected concentrations of poverty, and**

> **Comparing the relative impact of the different ways to improve conditions for current residents to see if they are actively reducing segregation.**

---

[23] Details of your local area's progress against floor targets is available at www.neighbourhood.gov.uk/fti.asp

[24] Hou F, Myles J. 'Neighbourhood inequality, neighbourhood affluence and population health'. Social Science & Medicine 2005; 60: 1557–1569.

The Sustainable Development Research Network report[25], commissioned for this Strategy, backed by evidence from Scotland and an Environment Agency report,[26] highlights another increasingly important area of inequality:

"Poor local environmental quality and differing ease of access to environmental goods and services have a detrimental effect on the quality of life experienced by deprived communities and socially excluded groups and can reinforce deprivation if not tackled alongside access to employment, health and tackling crime."

The research draws together the emerging evidence for the cause and impact of environmental inequalities for twenty one issues, such as graffiti and vandalism, access to transport services, and air pollution. It shows how complex and varied the patterns of environmental inequality are, and demonstrates that it is real problem within the UK affecting the most deprived communities. The research also draws attention to the need for further work on the causes, cost and effectiveness of policy interventions.

From evaluations of Community Strategies, the Government was already aware that these were key issues in deprived areas so it has established a new floor target to ensure cleaner, safer and greener public spaces and improve the quality of the built environment in deprived areas and across the country by 2008. Programmes within the Cleaner, Safer, Greener Communities priorities[27] tackle these issues, but we need more research on which approaches to tackling environmental inequality are likely to be the most effective.[28]

> **The Government will fund further research on the causes of environmental inequality and the effectiveness of measures to tackle it in order to establish the best ways to tackle these issues in communities**

For some issues, it is possible to map links between deprivation and a poor local environment, such as access to green space, fly-tipping and air quality using recently produced statistical data.

[25] PSI, Lucas et al, 2004, 'Environmental and Social Justice: Rapid Research and Evidence Review' at www.sd-research.org.uk

[26] Walker, G.P, Mitchell, G., Fairburn, J. and Smith, G., 2003, 'Environmental Quality and Social Deprivation. Phase II: National Analysis of Flood Hazard, IPC Industries and Air Quality'. R&D Project Record E2-067/1/PR1, The Environment Agency, Bristol.

[27] www.cleanersafergreener.gov.uk

[28] More details on tackling environmental inequality are available from a policy and practice guide at www.renewal.net which we will update in line with this strategy, with further advice available at local level from the Environment Agency, for example on flooding, the Health Protection Agency, for example on chemical exposure, and the Integrated Agency, for example rural access to services.

Map showing 2001 background NO$_2$ levels and boundaries of Neighbourhood Renewal Fund areas.

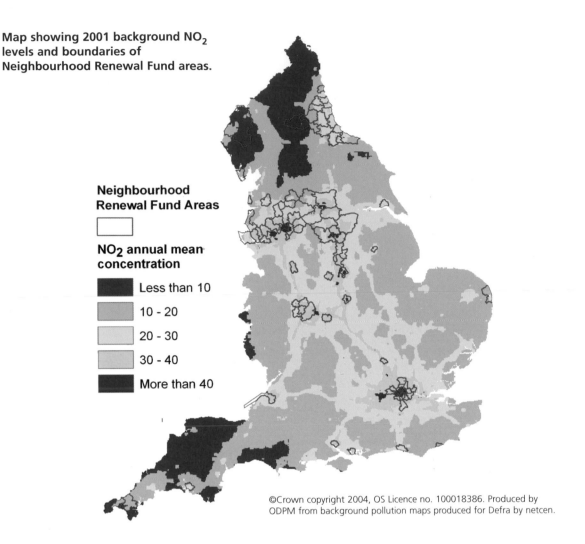

Neighbourhood Renewal Fund Areas

NO$_2$ annual mean concentration

Less than 10

10 - 20

20 - 30

30 - 40

More than 40

©Crown copyright 2004, OS Licence no. 100018386. Produced by ODPM from background pollution maps produced for Defra by netcen.

The Government will tackle poor air quality in line with the outcomes of a review of the Air Quality Strategy and by advising local authorities to incorporate air quality action plans into their local transport plans where transport is a contributory factor.

But across the range of local environmental issues, we need to ensure that action is focussed on the areas most in need. We already have a comprehensive system of statutory designations which allows us to identify and protect the most fragile natural environments, but we do not have a system for identifying the poorest quality local environments which need most enhancement to improve people's health and quality of life. The Government plans to put this system in place and use that as a basis for encouraging all local service providers through the local authorities and LSPs to focus on these areas, in consultation with the communities who live there, for example through Local Area Agreements.

> ❯ **While we carry out further research to help identify the areas with the worst local environment, the Government will in the short term focus on improving the environment in the areas already identified as most deprived by the Index of Multiple Deprivation.**

Issues of inequality are at the heart of the Government's agenda. It will use the following initiatives to incentivise the tackling of inequalities locally, in a joined-up way:

	Health inequalities	Road Safety	Education and child care	Fuel Poverty

ISSUE	In some parts of the country, average mortality rates are the same now as in the 1950s	Children living in the most deprived areas in England are five times more likely to be killed in a road accident as children in more affluent areas	Ensuring a high standard of education for all, and suitable child care facilities	Fuel poverty; a combination of poor energy efficiency in homes and low incomes
	The Government's Spearhead Primary Care Trusts (PCTs) will address health inequalities with additional resources and new programmes such as the 'Healthier Communities Collaborative' from 2006. We are also giving PCTs the means to tackle health inequalities and improve health by: funding to give greater priority to areas of high health need, new investment in primary care facilities for some 50 per cent of the population by 2008 with a focus on the most deprived areas of our communities, and development of a tool to assess local health and wellbeing that will help PCTs and local authorities jointly plan services and check on progress in reducing inequalities, called a health and well being equity audit.	There are a number of actions and programmes underway to improve road safety for all those living in deprived areas, which contribute towards meeting DfT's national target. Amongst these the Government's £17.6 million Neighbourhood Road Safety Initiative is supporting fifteen local authorities in the most deprived areas to tackle their high number of road casualties.	The Government's strategy for bringing about sustainable improvement in schools shows how Government will deliver on its key commitments to raise achievement in schools and address differences in achievement that arise between genders, ethnic groups, social classes and place (most and least deprived areas). The Government has also set out its commitment to invest in childcare, early education and work life balance so that families are able to secure the best start in life for their children.	The decent homes standard requires that homes have effective heating and insulation. In the private sector, Defra's Warm Front programme will be strengthened, so by 2010, fuel poverty in England for vulnerable households will be practically eradicated.
	www.dh.gov.uk/PublicationsAndStatistics/	www.nrsi.org.uk	www.dfes.gov.uk/achievingsuccess/download.shtml www.hm-treasury.gov.uk/pre_budget_report/prebud_pbr04/assoc_docs/prebud_pbr04_adchildcare.cfm	www.odpm.gov.uk and www.defra.gov.uk/environment/energy/hees/

Photo source: 3rd Avenue

Housing	Jobs	Transport and Accessibility	Crime
	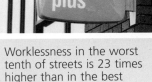		
Affordability and homelessness	Worklessness in the worst tenth of streets is 23 times higher than in the best tenth[29]	People, for example, the elderly or the disabled, not being able to access the services they need[30]	Over half of all crime (based on 2003/04 Home Office statistics) takes place in just 23 per cent of Local Authority areas – the 88 most deprived areas in England. Heroin, crack and cocaine users are responsible for 50 per cent of crimes such as burglary, vehicle crime, shop lifting and theft
We have doubled investment in social housing since 1997. The Government: – will help 80,000 into low cost home ownership by 2010 – will help deliver 1.1m new homes in the wider South East to 2016 – intends to set a national market affordability goal by the end of 2005, and – will focus on halving numbers living in temporary accommodation by 2010.	JobCentre Plus managers will be increasingly empowered to tailor targeted policies for particularly disadvantaged groups or areas. Support through the work of Business in the Community will help supply jobs in some of the most deprived areas. The Government will support: – measures to promote self-employment in deprived areas – more emphasis on mixed communities to reduce concentrations of worklessness most deprived areas – measures to promote self-employment in deprived areas, and – more emphasis on mixed communities to reduce concentrations of worklessness.	Accessibility planning[31] sets a framework for identifying and tackling the barriers faced by people, particularly those from disadvantaged groups and areas in accessing jobs and essential services. Measures to improve accessibility can also contribute to improving the local environment and quality of life. Accessibility planning considers the needs of those in both urban and rural areas. Local authorities that produce Local Transport Plans (LTPs)[32] will have to produce accessibility strategies as part of them from July 2005 (to be finalised in March 2006). These strategies should set out an authority's vision and objectives for accessibility and include local targets for accessibility improvements. LTPs can help improve access to the countryside by including statutory Rights of Way Improvement Plans. Many LTPs refer to development of travel plan initiatives at NHS facilities (for staff, patients and visitors). All schools in England will be required to have a school travel plan by 2010, as set out in the 'Travelling to School' initiative The Government is providing £50 million over 2004-2006 to support this project.	The Government will focus on and prioritise policing, including neighbourhood policing, in the highest crime areas which are also the most deprived (an 85 per cent correlation in 2003/04). The Drug Interventions Programme, launched in April 2003, is a 'beginning-to-end support programme' aimed at getting drug misusers out of crime and into treatment. It operates in those areas with the highest levels of acquisitive crime which closely correspond to the poorest communities.
www.odpm.gov.uk/odpm/five yearstrategy/homes_for_all.htm	www.dwp.gov.uk/lifeevent/ workage/index.asp	www.dft.gov.uk/stellent/groups/ dft_localtrans/documents/page/ dft_localtrans_504005.hcsp	

29 ODPM, 2004, 'Jobs and Enterprise in Deprived Areas'.
30 ODPM, 2003, 'Making the connections'.
31 DfT, 2004, 'Full Guidance on Accessibility Planning'.
32 DfT, 2004, 'Full Guidance on Local Transport Plans: Second Edition'.

Photo source: 3rd Avenue

3. Providing opportunity for all nationally

Not all deprived people live in deprived areas, and some of the most deprived are rootless, with little attachment to any community. We need to make sure that both for people and places, we are tackling the key drivers of deprivation that risk pushing people into a spiral of decline.

In England, the Social Exclusion Unit's (SEU) report 'Breaking the cycle: taking stock of progress and priorities'[33] took stock of the impact of Government policy since 1997 and assessed the national state on deprivation. It showed that the Government's investment and reform programme has delivered real progress. For example, some of society's most deep-rooted social problems like rough-sleeping have been turned around. But it also showed that services need to work harder helping those who are still at risk – often the most vulnerable. It also highlighted the need for continued action to prevent disadvantage being passed from one generation to another. The report identified five specific key drivers of social exclusion that need to be tackled: worklessness, homelessness, low educational attainment, health inequalities and crime.

Transforming public services for all

This is part of the Government's wider drive to create more responsive and personalised public services. It is often the most disadvantaged who are worst served by a 'standard' service. Services designed around users will be better placed to help those with complicated and multiple needs. With this in mind, the SEU's new work programme is looking at how mainstream services could work better to meet the needs of the bottom 10 per cent, in order to improve life chances for the most disadvantaged. In particular it will focus on:

Source: 3rd Avenue

> young adults with troubled lives

> disadvantaged adults of working age (particularly those with poor basic skills, disadvantaged ethnic groups and those with health problems)

> excluded older people, and

> disadvantaged people who move frequently.

It will also look at cross cutting work on how assets affect life chances and how social exclusion can be tackled through new technologies.

[33] ODPM, 2004, 'Breaking the cycle: taking stock of progress and priorities' at www.crimereduction.gov.uk/socialexclusion01.htm

The UK Government believes that, for those able to work, employment is the best route out of poverty, because it offers each individual the chance to fulfil his or her potential, boosts their self-confidence, and contributes to social justice. So an effective labour market policy helps ensure economic and social benefits accrue to the many rather than the few.

The Government's policy approach to worklessness can be grouped under three themes:

➤ providing support by ensuring the benefit system helps and encourages those on benefits to return to work – while recognising that there are those who, perhaps because of caring responsibilities, disability or health, cannot be required to look for work

➤ ensuring work pays through the introduction of a minimum wage and tax credits, and

➤ reducing barriers to work by a range of means, including improving skills and access to childcare

Two groups in society will be the focus of Government support in the coming years: young people and the elderly.

The Government's long-term goal is to halve the number of children in relative low-income households between 1998/99 and 2010/11, on the way to eradicating child poverty by 2020, shared by the Department for Work and Pensions and HM Treasury. The strategy involves:

➤ ensuring decent family incomes

➤ helping parents who can work into work

➤ support for parents in their parenting role, and

➤ delivering excellent public services.

The Government has succeeded in arresting and reversing the long-term trend of rising child poverty and is broadly on track to meet its target to reduce the number of children in relative low-income households by 2004/05.

The Government is also tackling poverty through personal tax and benefit changes which focus on the poorest pensioners.

Pensioners have recently benefited from the Pension Credit, which offers a minimum weekly income, and rises in the Basic State Pension in lines with prices or 2.5 per cent (whichever is higher). Public pension spending is projected to remain stable over the next 50 years, fluctuating between 4.9 per cent and 5.4 per cent of Gross Domestic Product.

Targeted support is also given to help with living expenses, winter fuel payments and council tax bills. Those over 60 are also entitled to free prescriptions, free eyesight tests and travel concessions, while those over 75 receive free television licences. For the years ahead, the UK has established a Pensions Commission to analyse the likely future for UK pensions provision and retirement saving.

The Government's annual report, 'Opportunity for All'[34] sets out the Government's evidence-based strategy for tackling poverty and social exclusion. This incorporates a set of indicators measuring its own effectiveness.

3. The global dimension: a fairer world

We have created a relatively good quality of life in this country for most of us but we now realise that this may have been at the expense of communities elsewhere in the world.

Rich and poor worlds cannot co-exist without dramatic consequences. In 2000, states facing stability challenges contained just over 1.2 billion people living on less than one dollar a day, and 65 million of the 114 million children of primary school age who did not attend school.

In the past our efforts have concentrated on dealing with consequences of instability and responding to crises. But more effective international responses to reduce risks of instability – and thereby prevent crises – are possible. The Prime Minister's Strategy Unit's recent report[35] argues that all countries are potentially at risk of instability and sets out practical steps to make prevention real. The heart of prevention is long-term sustained investment in boosting country capacity and resilience to manage risks and deal with shocks in ways which boost rather than undermine natural and human capital.

Part of the prevention strategy is for the international community to take more responsbility for its own actions. Changing weather patterns and climate variability are already contributing to risks of instability in a number of vulnerable countries. Food and water scarcity, changes in land use and natural disasters and environmental migration can all play a part in escalating tensions; and environmental stresses have been linked to political tensions and violent conflicts in a number of specific cases.

Creating a fairer world is essential for the UK's own stability and prosperity. As a wealthy country, the UK is well placed to help developing countries. Tackling global poverty is a priority for the UK, and our actions are framed by the Millennium Development Goals (MDGs) and other associated international agreements. In this context, the UK can set out its goals in a way that tries to ensure human rights, democracy and good governance and, where aid is given, countries are empowered to decide their own priorities and needs.

In our international development assistance we follow an approach tailored to the differing contexts of individual countries. We direct attention to the underlying and longer-term factors that affect the opportunities for reform in different countries, as well as factors that more directly affect the incentives and capacity for change. We consider the role of agents, institutions and structural issues. This allows the Government to acquire a longer-term perspective, and to better capitalise on short- and medium-term opportunities to support strategic change.

---

[34] DWP, 2004, 'Opportunity for All', at www.dwp.gov.uk/ofa/index.asp
[35] PMSU, 2005, 'Investing in Prevention: An International Strategy to manage Risks of Instability and Improve Crisis Response'.

Countries which are democratic, with governments that respect the rights of and are responsive to the needs of their people, and which observe the rule of law, are more likely to achieve sustainable development. The Government seeks to promote human rights, democracy and good political, environmental and economic governance through its foreign policy.

Bisaland, Burkina Faso
© *Crispin Hughes/Panos Pictures*

A key element of this agenda is to encourage civil society and broader public participation in decision-making; to promote freedom of information, including support for a free media; and to promote access to justice and the rule of law. In this context, the UK government is a strong advocate of environmental democracy, defined as the three strands of Principle 10 of the Rio Declaration (1992) which seeks to address inequalities of access to information, public participation in decision-making and access to justice in environmental matters. The UK is a founding partner of the Partnership for Principle 10, an international partnership open to governments, international organisations and civil society groups established at the World Summit on Sustainable Development (WSSD) in 2002, which aims to enhance and accelerate Principle 10 at the national level.

The UK announced its commitments to the partnership in June 2004. The UK Government will continue to promote the aims of the Partnership through the FCO network of environmental attachés overseas, and report on the progress made against the commitments at the annual Committee of the Whole meetings.

The international principles and standards of "environmental democracy" (access to information, public participation, and access to justice) set out in the UNECE (United Nations Economic Commission for Europe) Aarhus Convention have become embedded in the EU and UK systems of governance. For the future, our priority will be to encourage the building of capacity and the development of good practice in the application of these principles and standards elsewhere in the UNECE region, particularly in EECCA (Eastern European, Caucasus and Central Asian) countries, as well as on the wider global stage.

To achieve good governance we need to eliminate corruption. The Government will build support for ratification of the UN Convention against Corruption, including through strengthening anti-corruption capacity in developing countries.

> ⟩ **To reinforce this, the Government will continue our bilateral and multilateral support for strengthening anti-corruption capacity in developing countries**

We also remain committed to extending the Extractives Industries Transparency Initiative, (EITI) which seeks to increase the transparency of payments by extractives (oil, gas, and minerals) companies to governments, as well as the transparency of the revenues received by governments. Revenues from this sector should be an important engine for economic growth and social development in developing countries. However, the lack of transparency of these revenues can lead to conflict, corruption, and poverty. The EITI also seeks to ensure that civil society is involved in the analysis of payment figures and in discussions on how they might be used. It therefore seeks to increase the quality of governance of those resources.

Government spending on overseas development is governed by the International Development Act of 2002, which requires funds to be spent for poverty reduction, either through sustainable development or increasing the welfare of a population.[36] The Department for International Development (DFID) has made the Millennium Development Goals (MDGs) the focus of its work.

However, the MDGs will not be met in many areas of the world, unless significant changes are made to the amount of financial resources available for international development, and the way in which they are used.

The Government is committed to achieving the United Nations 0.7 per cent target for ODA as a proportion of gross national income (GNI). Under the terms of the Spending Review 2004, total UK official development assistance (ODA) will rise from £4.1 billion in 2004/05 to £6.5 billion by 2007/08. The UK is making progress towards the UN 0.7 per cent target for official development assistance (ODA) as a proportion of gross national income. On current plans this will rise to 0.39 per cent in 2005/06 and 0.47 per cent in 2007/08. The Government wishes to continue to raise UK ODA at the rate of growth achieved in 2007/08 in the aid ratio, which on this timetable would rise beyond 0.5 per cent after 2008 and reach 0.7 per cent by 2013.

Bisaland, Burkina Faso
© Crispin Hughes/Panos Pictures

A flexible approach to raising aid volumes should be adopted, and the UK will work with partners to encourage international agreement on a framework in which all donors can contribute in different ways. One way would be through the International Finance Facility (IFF), proposed in January 2003, by HM Treasury and DFID. The IFF is the most advanced proposal to frontload aid and would immediately provide a predictable source of resources needed to reach the MDGs ahead of 2015. This would double development aid by raising an additional $50 billion a year for the world's poorest countries in the years to 2015.

The IFF, which has received broad support from emerging markets, developing countries, international institutions, faith communities, non-governmental organisations and business, could provide the critical mass of additional and predictable funding needed to make lasting progress in all these areas, tackling the causes rather than the symptoms of poverty.

The UK is contributing to the target on slum dwellers through programmes to upgrade slums and build the capacity of municipal governments in India, and has provided £1 million for the City Community Challenge Fund in Zambia and Uganda, to reduce urban poverty. The UK is also the largest single donor to the Cities Alliance and DFID sits on its Consultative Group.

As well as increasing the volume, development assistance must be delivered and used in the most effective ways. The UK will work to:

❯ **Improve aid relationships with partners so that:**

    ❯ **financial resources are aligned with priorities set out in country-owned national Poverty Reduction and Development Strategies**

[36] Funds may also be used for humanitarian assistance and for development in UK Overseas Territories.

> ❯ **donor programmes and procedures are harmonised to reduce duplication among donors and help reduce the burden on partner countries**

> ❯ **financial resources are more predictable – enabling partners to plan ahead and engage on longer term programmes, and**

> ❯ **there is a more equal partnership, with country-led approaches where programmes build on partner development priorities, where conditions of aid are jointly agreed and based on outcomes rather than activities, and where there is mutual accountability between donor and recipient.**

❯ **Promote good governance to reduce waste and corruption**

❯ **Improve policy coherence for development – ensuring that policies, for example, in trade, migration and finance, support development rather than undermine it**

❯ **Use an appropriate mix of aid instruments, including general and sectoral budget support, technical assistance, projects and funds**

❯ **Explore ways of engaging more effectively in fragile states**

❯ **Support developing countries to improve the opportunities for environmental sustainability to be integrated into poverty reduction strategies and programmes, and encourage other donors to do the same**

In 2001 the UK fully untied its bilateral aid. This means that our aid is not conditional on contracts for UK companies. We encourage other donors to do the same. Untied aid leads to goods and services focused on developing countries' priorities; it provides new opportunities for developing countries' private sectors.

Our integrated approach for creating sustainable communities and a fairer world

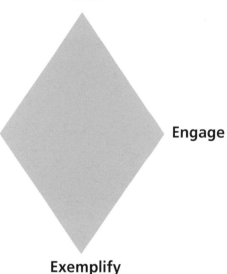

Enable

- Academy for Sustainable Communities
- Research environmental inequality
- Better information on local neighbourhoods
- Map out areas of priority for local environmental improvement
- Provide capacity building on community engagement

Encourage

- Planning system
- Safer and Stronger Communities Fund
- Comprehesive Performance Assessment
- Big Lottery Fund
- Targeted support for deprived areas
- Clean Neighbourhoods and Environment Bill
- Overseas Development Aid
- International Finance Facility

Engage

- "Community Action 2020: Together We Can"
- Community contribution to Sustainable Community Strategies, Local Transport Plans, Neighbourhood and parish plans
- Neighbourhood contracts
- Community Empowerment Networks
- Statements of Community Involvement
- Tackling local health and environmental inequalities

Exemplify

- Sustainable Communities vision
- Local Area Agreements
- Shared Priorities

4. Measuring our progress

Earlier in this chapter, we mentioned how Local Strategic Partnerships will choose sets of indicators most relevant to them to measure progress. At a national level, the UK Government use the indicators listed below to measure progress in England against these issues: when we report against them, we will take into account the rate of progress for different social groups, and the rate of progress in the most deprived areas, compared with the rest of England.

> ❯ **This means that the Government will have a stronger set of sustainable development indicators for addressing social, economic and environmental inequalities at local level**

Indicators to be used to report progress will include all indicators within the UK Framework set that are relevant to sustainable communities and in addition other indicators relevant to the priorities of the UK Government Strategy:

Society

> **Active community participation*:** informal and formal volunteering at least once a month

> **Crime*:** crime survey and recorded crime for (a) vehicles (b) domestic burglary (c) violence

> **Fear of crime:** (a) car theft (b) burglary (c) physical attack

Employment and poverty

> **Employment*:** people of working age in employment

> **Workless households*:** population living in workless households (a) children (b) working age

> **Economically inactive:** people of working age who are economically inactive

> **Childhood poverty*:** children in relative low-income households (a) before housing costs (b) after housing costs

> **Young adults:** 16-19 year-olds not in employment, education or training

> **Pensioner poverty*:** pensioners in relative low-income households (a) before housing costs (b) after housing costs

> **Pension provision*:** working age people contributing to a non-state pension in at least three years out of the last four

Education

> **Education*:** 19 year olds with level 2 qualifications and above

> **Sustainable development education:** *(to be developed to monitor the impact of formal learning on knowledge and awareness of sustainable development)*

Health

> **Health inequality*:** (a) infant mortality (by social-economic group) (b) life expectancy (by area) for men and women

> **Healthy life expectancy:** healthy life expectancy (a) men (b) women

> **Mortality rates:** death rates from (a) circulatory disease and (b) cancer, below 75 years and for areas with the worst health and deprivation indicators, and (c) suicides

> **Smoking:** prevalence of smoking (a) all adults (b) 'routine and manual' socio-economic groups

> **Childhood obesity:** prevalence of obesity in 2-10 year olds

> **Diet:** people consuming five or more portions of fruit and vegetables per day and in low income households

Mobility and access

> **Mobility*:** (a) number of trips per person by mode (b) distance travelled per person per year by broad trip purpose

> **Getting to school:** how children get to school

> **Accessibility:** access to key services

> **Road accidents:** number of people and children killed or seriously injured

Social justice/Environmental equality

> **Social justice*:** *(social measures to be developed)*

> **Environmental equality*:** *(environmental measures to be developed)*

> **Local environment quality:** *(to be developed using information from the Local Environmental Quality Survey of England)*
> **Satisfaction in local area:** households satisfied with the quality of the places in which they live (a) overall (b) in deprived areas (c) non-decent homes
> **Air quality and health:** (a) annual levels of particles and ozone (b) days when air pollution is moderate or higher

Housing

> **Housing conditions:** (a) social sector homes below the decent homes standard (b) vulnerable households in the private sector in homes below the decent homes standard
> **Households living in fuel poverty:** (a) pensioners (b) households with children (c) disabled/long-term sick
> **Homelessness:** (a) rough sleepers and (b) households in temporary accommodation (i) total (ii) households with children
> **Land recycling:** (a) new dwellings built on previously developed land or through conversions (b) all new development on previously developed land
> **Dwelling density:** average density of new housing

Wellbeing

> **Wellbeing*:** *(to be developed)*

International

> **UK International assistance:** Net Official Development Assistance (a) per cent of Gross National Income (comparison with selected countries) (b) per capita (comparison with selected countries)
> In addition, as set out in Chapter 1, we will provide access to indicators for international sustainable development on the UK Government's sustainable development website.

Other contextual indicators

> **Economic output*:** Gross Domestic Product
> **Productivity:** UK output per worker
> **Investment:** (a) total investment (b) social investment relative to GDP
> **Demography:** population and population of working age
> **Households and dwelling stock:** households, single person households and dwelling stock

* Indicator is included in the UK Framework Indicators

Key contributions

Each key Government department has identified some of their high-level contributions to delivering this strategy. All departments will produce a Sustainable Development Action Plan by the end of 2005.

Office of the Deputy Prime Minister

1. Creating sustainable communities that embody the principles of sustainable development at the local level.

2. Providing homes for all, while protecting and enhancing the environment.

3. Working to give communities more power and say in their decisions that affect them; and working to improve governance at all levels so that we can work at the right level to get things done.

4. Creating cleaner, safer, greener agenda: to make public spaces cleaner safer and greener and to improve the quality of the built environment in deprived areas and across the country by 2008.

5. Promoting sustainable, high quality design and construction, to reduce waste and improve resource efficiency, and promoting more sustainable buildings.

6. Putting sustainable development at the heart of the planning system, as set out in Planning Policy Statement 1 'Delivering Sustainable Development'.

Department of Work and Pensions

1. Ensuring the best start for all children, and ending child poverty by 2020.

2. Promoting work as the best form of welfare for people of working age, while protecting the position of those in greatest need.

3. Combating poverty and promoting security and independence in retirement for today's and tomorrow's pensioners.

4. Improving rights and opportunities for disabled people in a fair and inclusive society.

5. Ensuring that we continue to build sustainability into all our activities, and reporting on our progress.

Department for Transport

1. Developing cleaner fuels and vehicles: 2002 Powering Future Vehicles (PFV) Strategy and the New Vehicle Technology Fund (spending in excess of £100 million per annum); eco-labelling proposal being considered by Low Carbon Vehicle Partnership.

2. Ambitious targets in PFV Strategy to increase the number of new sales of low emitting cars (by 2012, 10 per cent emitting $100g/cm^3$ or less) and the number of low carbon buses (by 2012, 600 or more buses coming into operation per annum will emit 30 per cent or less below 2002 average carbon emissions).

3. Reducing aviation emissions: pushing at EU and international level for the inclusion of aviation emissions in emissions trading schemes.

4. Sustainable freight strategy: including funding for Road Haulage Modernisation Fund and developing Freight Quality Partnerships. Lorry road user charging is due to be delivered by 2007-08.

5. New round of local transport plans: integrating air quality action plans and setting clear objectives for accessibility planning.

6. School travel: working with DfES to implement the Travelling to School action plan, including the introduction of travel plans in all schools by 2010.

Department for Culture, Media and Sport

1. Through the input of our sectors into changing behaviours: by example, in the maintenance of our buildings, and by our support for exhibitions on relevant subjects in Museums, libraries and galleries, and through the arts.

2. Through the input of the Commission for Architecture and the Built Environment (CABE) and English Heritage to the built and historic environment, in designing and greening public spaces (e.g. turning waste ground into parks).

3. Through trying to influence the input of tourism to the economy, in reacting to climate change, and in promoting the practise of sustainable tourism, for example through the Travel Foundation with the FCO.

4. Through our support of initiatives to improve general health and reduce obesity by encouraging participation in sport and active leisure pursuits, in adults and in children.

5. Through our work with young people in providing alternative activities to involvement in crime, and raising awareness of their involvement in their communities, and in providing volunteering opportunities, through influencing the staging of major events (such as the London 2012 Olympics bid and Proms in the Park).

Foreign and Commonwealth Office

1. To deliver the Government's international sustainable development objectives making the most of our network of diplomatic posts overseas. The FCO's Sustainable Development Strategy, to be launched on 14 March, will set out how the FCO will do this. A complementary Strategy on Human Rights, Democracy and Governance will be published later in the year.

2. Promoting human rights, democracy and good political, environmental and economic governance overseas.

3. Delivering on the two WSSD commitments on which the FCO has the overall lead: promoting environmental governance and human rights; and international sustainable development governance. In March 2005 we will publish delivery plans (agreed across Whitehall), setting out priority actions – for the FCO, DFID, DEFRA, and our diplomatic posts overseas – to meet these commitments.

4. Contributing to tackling climate change. Helping to ensure that the international debate on climate change is re-energised through the UK's presidencies of the G8 and EU in 2005, and that both result in concrete actions.

5. Launching a new Sustainable Development Programme under the FCO's Global Opportunities Fund in April 2005. This will provide £5 million a year for local, national, regional and international projects. Priority themes will include transparency, information, participation and access to justice; core human rights priorities (including combating torture, abolishing the death penalty and promoting child rights); and natural resource management (including sustainable forest management and reduction of illegal logging, biodiversity and sustainable tourism).

Department for Environment, Food and Rural Affairs

1. Providing international leadership on climate change underpinned by domestic action – energy efficiency, and climate change review and elimination of fuel poverty.

2. Putting sustainable development into practice through implementation of the Sustainable Food and Farming Strategy, animal health and welfare, development of sustainable fisheries policy.

3. Establishing a new integrated agency and marine agency for sustainable management of natural resources at land and sea.

4. Developing programmes for decoupling environmental degradation from economic growth, including funding of Business and Resource Efficiency and Waste Fund, the waste strategy review; and our work on more sustainable consumption and production.

5. Building bilateral Sustainable Development dialogues with a small number of rapidly developing countries (initially India and China) to build on, and provide a framework for, existing country-level activities as well as identify new areas of collaboration.

6. Increasing focus on improving the local environment by understanding better and tackling environmental inequalities and joint work with the Department of Health.

7. Co-ordination of the development of this strategy including publication of the UK sustainable development indicators.

Department of Trade and Industry

1. Working closely with Defra, DfT and a wide range of others to implement the Energy White Paper: 'Our Energy Future – Creating a Low Carbon Economy' which sets out a strategy for delivering sustainable, reliable and affordable energy supplies through competitive markets. The Strategy puts the UK on a path to a 60 per cent reduction in carbon emissions by 2050, with real progress by 2020, as well as mapping out an approach to ensure we have sufficient – and sufficiently diverse – energy sources in the future. In the nearer term the aims are to:
   - reduce greenhouse gas emissions, in line with our Kyoto commitment, by 12.5 per cent from 1990 levels in 2008-12; and move towards a 20 per cent reduction in carbon dioxide emissions from 1990 levels by 2010, and

   - increase the proportion of UK electricity supplied from renewable energy sources to ten per cent in 2010, consistent with our wider goals for affordable and reliable energy supplies.

2. Contributing to sustainable development worldwide through a successful outcome on the Doha Development Agenda, especially the trade and environment and trade and development elements, and the inclusion of sustainable development in EU bilateral trade agreements.

3. Increasing the business contribution to sustainable development and de-couple economic growth from environmental impacts by:
   - promoting corporate responsibility in all areas of business activity, including in local communities and internationally

   - promoting sustainable consumption and production, including through an eco-design academy and a sector sustainability challenge, and

   - integrating sustainability into other DTI policy areas and business support.

Department of Health

1. The National Health Service (NHS) as a Corporate Citizen. This has been identified as one of the NHS Chief Executive's five new priorities for the next ten years. As part of that work we will fund the Sustainable Development Commission Healthy Futures programme to develop the capacity of NHS organisations to act as good corporate citizens.

2. Food and Health Action Plan. We will work with the farming and food industries to coordinate action, including action to take forward policies in this Strategy, through a Food and Health Action Plan to be published in early 2005 fulfilling the commitment to such a plan in the Strategy for Sustainable Farming and Food. This will be backed up with wider action in the Food Standards Agency Strategic Plan.

3. Transport and Health. Following evaluation, we will build on the Sustainable Travel Towns pilots to develop guidance for local authorities, PCTs and others on whole-town approaches to shifting travel from cars to walking, cycling and public transport.

4. Healthy Sustainable Communities. We will extend the current healthy communities initiative to more deprived communities from 2006, and we will use collaborative techniques to support action through local partnerships. We are also giving Primary Care Trusts the means to tackle health inequalities and improve health.

5. Health Impact. Department of Health representatives located in the regions will lead the work with regional and local government and the NHS to ensure that regional partner policies and activities take account of their health impact, e.g. housing, transport, planning, employment, education and skills, environment, rural affairs, crime and community safety.

Department for International Development

1. Working in developing countries with a wide range of stakeholders to help in the preparation and implementation of national strategies for poverty reduction.

2. Developing sectoral policies and plans for meeting specific UK commitments arising from the World Summit on Sustainable Development.

3. Ensuring our own development support is evaluated for social and environmental impacts.

4. Supporting key multilateral institutions that provide the information, policy forum, and/or resource mobilisation to tackle global sustainability issues.

5. Supporting developing countries' participation in international sustainable development initiatives.

6. Working towards national and international policy coherence for development, ensuring that policies in trade, migration, finance, etc, support development and do not undermine it.

7. Ensuring that our activities are aligned with developing countries priorities and harmonised with activities of other donors.

Home Office

1. Reduce crime by 15 per cent and further in high crime areas by 2007-08.

2. Reassure the public, reducing fear of crime and anti-social behaviour and building confidence in the Criminal Justice System without compromising fairness.

3. Increase voluntary and community engagement, especially amongst those at risk of social exclusion.

4. Reduce race inequalities and build community cohesion.

5. Produce a Departmental Sustainable Procurement Strategy by 1 December 2005.

HM Treasury

1. Building a strong and productive economy and a fair society where there is opportunity and security for all.

2. A transparent public expenditure delivery framework, based on public service agreements (PSAs) that focus on delivering public services in areas integral to achieving Sustainable Development in the UK, such as reducing and eliminating child poverty and reducing unemployment.

3. Making use of the fiscal system, where appropriate, to tackle environmental externalities through developing further existing environmental taxes, such as the recent increases in the standard rate of landfill tax; creating tax incentives for cleaner technologies through enhanced capital allowances and adding an environmental dimension to transport taxation, for example through fuel duty differentials to encourage the use of cleaner fuels.

4. A commitment to strong local government, supporting local authorities in their delivery of key public services to all communities, for example through the introduction of the 3 year revenue and capital settlements, which will improve local authorities' ability to made sustainable long-term plans.

5. Continuing to meet relevant sustainable development objectives in public procurement by having a comprehensive and thoughtful approach to value for money and whole life costs of goods and services procured and by building relevant sustainability issues into the procurement process as early as possible.

Department for Education and Skills

1. The Building Schools for the Future programme will ensure that all new schools and academies will be models for sustainable development. The DfES is developing a school specific method of environmental assessment that will apply to all new school buildings.

2. The DfES is planning to launch in Spring 2005 a sustainable development framework for schools, a web-based service which will provide a one-stop shop for teachers, heads and governors who wish to make their schools more environmentally friendly and sustainable.

3. Both the Learning and Skills Council and the Higher Education Funding Council for England have recently published their own sustainable development strategies to promote and support sustainable development within the further and higher education sectors.

4. DfES wants to see sustainability literacy become a core competency for professionals in the work place. With Forum for the Future and professional bodies, the Department has set up the Sustainability Implementation Group to help colleges and universities to raise the profile of sustainability literacy in all curricula.

5. The DfES is funding a senior adviser on a fixed-term loan to the Sustainable Development Commission to help the Department achieve the objectives of its Action Plan, especially through effective liaison with NGOs, other departments and regional organisations.

Chapter 7
Ensuring It Happens

1. Delivery Matters

Strategies are worthless if they are not turned into action. Earlier chapters have set out what the Government needs to do. This chapter sets out how we plan to ensure we make the progress needed. The call for better delivery featured strongly in the responses to the consultation and we have taken up many of the ideas suggested.

Accountability and Responsibility

This is a UK Government-wide strategy covering all issues in England and those UK issues which are not the responsibility of devolved administrations. **Accountability** for its delivery ultimately rests with the Cabinet, and the Secretary of State for Environment, Food and Rural Affairs has a lead role. **Responsibility**, however, rests with everyone. The success of this strategy depends on the commitment and capacity of all Government departments, their agencies and other public bodies, including local authorities and those providing public services at regional and local level, communities, businesses and individuals.

" *Our biggest challenge in this new century is to take an idea that seems abstract – Sustainable Development – and turn it into a reality for all the world's people.*"

Kofi Annan, UN Secretary-General

The UK Government will also need to work closely and effectively with the devolved administrations to ensure delivery in areas where concerted action is necessary – for example in relation to climate change and renewable energy or where the actions of the UK Government have significant implications for the administrations of Scotland, Wales or Northern Ireland or vice versa.

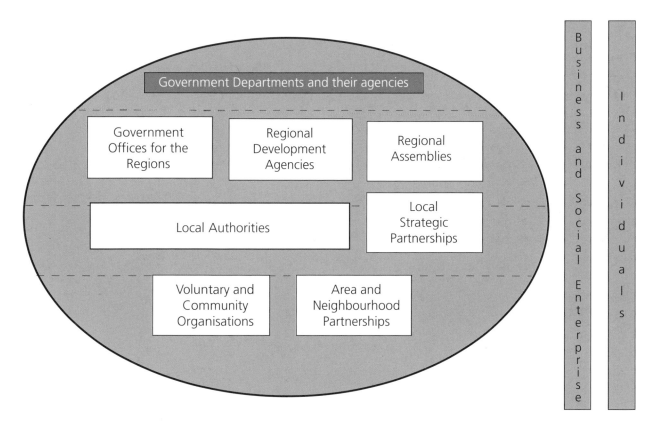

2. Strengthening national delivery

Sustainable development is a priority shared by all Government departments, although Defra holds the Public Service Agreement (PSA) target for its delivery. If Government is to achieve its objectives we need to increase the ability of and the incentives for all departments and the wider public sector to put sustainable development into practice. The following commitments will make a real difference:

▶ **All central Government departments and their executive agencies will produce focused sustainable development action plans based on this strategy by December 2005 and will report on their actions by December 2006, for example, in their departmental annual reports and regularly thereafter**

> ▶ **The Government will strengthen leadership capacity within departments and their agencies, for example by providing civil servants with better training in sustainable development**

> ▶ **The Government will set stretching targets for meeting its objectives on sustainable public procurement through a National Action Plan for Sustainable Procurement (see Chapter 3)**

> ▶ **The Government will ensure that an understanding of how to apply sustainable development principles is a key part of policy skills for the future and that all policies are properly appraised against the new principles of sustainable development**

> ▶ **The Government will strengthen the Sustainable Development Commission (SDC) and expand its role to act as an independent "watchdog" looking at Government's progress on this strategy**

> ▶ **The Government will use this strategy as the basis for integrating sustainable development into the 2006 spending review and later spending reviews which set Public Service Agreement targets and allocate resources**

Sustainable development is promoted and co-ordinated through a number of Ministerial and official level groups working across central Government.

In 2003 the Secretary of State for Environment, Food and Rural Affairs established a **Sustainable Development Task Force**, comprising Ministers and key stakeholders, whose remit was to advise on delivery of World Summit on Sustainable Development commitments and the development of this new strategy. Looking ahead, this Task Force will now help to advise on interdepartmental implementation of this strategy, including action on international work needed to deliver it.

The **Sustainable Development Commission** (SDC) was established in 2000 as a UK-wide advisory Non-Departmental Public Body with 21 Commissioners and a Chair. Its role is to act as the Government's independent advisor and "critical friend" on sustainable development. The Commission has developed its role and increased its influence across Government since 2000, so we need to ensure that it is resourced to respond to future challenges. Following a review of the SDC, we want to strengthen its capacity to ensure Government departments' policies optimise economic, social and environmental benefits.

> ▶ **The Government will give the SDC a new stronger role, with its own director and increased resources**

We will consider whether putting the SDC on a statutory footing as an executive rather than an advisory body would enhance this role further. We will also consider how the SDC's new watchdog role can best be carried out alongside its advisory role.

Policy Appraisal and Spending Reviews

The Government wants to put in place the right institutions and incentives, but we also need to make sure that sustainable development considerations are built into key stages of policy-making.

Sustainable development was a cross-cutting theme in the 2004 Spending Review which set Government resources and key national targets (PSA targets) for the years 2005-08.

> **This strategy will be used as a basis for integrating sustainable development into the 2006 Spending Review and future spending rounds which set PSA targets and allocate resources**

Since April 2004 all departments and their agencies have been required to include environmental and social costs and benefits, as well as economic costs and benefits, in the Regulatory Impact Assessments (RIAs) which they must produce and publish for all new proposals with significant public or private sector impacts. Environmental impacts include the impact on climate change, on which Defra has provided guidance[1]. The National Audit Office (NAO) reports to Parliament annually on RIAs and will from 2006 also look at sustainable development aspects.

In its earlier reports, the NAO found three main factors which characterised effective RIAs:

> starting the process early

> consulting effectively with those affected by the proposal, and

> analysing appropriately the likely costs and benefits of the proposal

This is even more true for sustainable development where the early identification of wider effects is crucial in seeking to devise more sustainable options, to maximise potential benefits and to reduce adverse impacts where these are unavoidable.

> **The Government will ensure that this message is reinforced at all levels across departments. The Government will also ensure that new case study guidance incorporates the latest thinking and techniques particularly on how to evaluate less tangible costs and benefits, such as the impact in different parts of the country and for different social groups on health, the environment, access to services, land use and natural resources so that issues of environmental inequality are addressed.**

Skills

No amount of guidance can be a substitute for giving people the skills they need to put sustainable development into practice. The Government has embarked on a major programme to equip the civil service with the skills it needs to address the challenges of the 21st century. A thorough understanding of how to apply sustainable development principles will need to be a key part of policy skills for the future as will the ability to engage the wider public in the development and implementation of new ideas.

Sustainable development is already being integrated more effectively into the Government's 'Centre for Management and Policy Studies' (CMPS). CMPS has recently piloted a new workshop for senior civil servants on how sustainable development can help to deliver better policy-making. The CMPS's work will be incorporated into the new National School of Government, created to help Government organisations in the UK and internationally to be more professional and to offer better value services to Ministers and to the public they serve.

---

[1] See www.defra.gov.uk/corporate/regulat/ria/envguide/ccrisk/index.htm

> **The Government will embed sustainable development into the curriculum of the National School of Government[2], to be launched in the first half of 2005 in areas such as policy-making, strategic leadership, programme and project management and the behavioural aspects of management development**

Defra is developing toolkits and awareness raising materials in partnership with Futerra and Forum for the Future to help its staff deliver sustainable development better through all of its policies and services. Once trialled within Defra, these will be made available to all Government departments and other groups as part of a resource centre available through the sustainable development website.

Government Operations

We want the public sector to be a leading exponent of sustainable development. This was a key reason for our decision to introduce the 'Framework for Sustainable Development on the Government Estate'. This framework sets targets to be met by Government Departments and their executive agencies in a number of areas including water and energy use, and procurement.

Reports of progress against these targets are published each year (at www.sustainable-development.gov.uk) and they demonstrate that performance, although improving, is still patchy. We want departments to do better and to set an example for the rest of the public sector and businesses.

> **The Government is reviewing the framework, to be sure that we adopt the right approach for the future, and will make proposals during 2005 for achieving a significant change in its own performance**

In 2004, for the first time, the annual report on Sustainable Development in Government, which sets out departments' performance against targets in the Framework for Sustainable Development in the Government Estate[3], was based on an analysis by independent consultants. In future, such reports will be wholly independent of Government.

Statutory duties

Some public bodies already have statutory duties in relation to sustainable development, such as the National Assembly for Wales and the Greater London Assembly. These take different forms. Our priority is to ensure that they have clear guidance on the implications of those duties based on the revised principles set out in Chapter 1.

> **By 2006 the Government will issue clear guidance on how existing bodies with a statutory duty linked to sustainable development should take account of this strategy**

We have also considered whether a general statutory duty on all, or the most important, public bodies to promote sustainable development would lead to clearer responsibilities and improved delivery of our sustainable development goals. It is difficult to attribute changes to the existence of a statutory duty alone and we must consider the cumulative impact of many statutory duties upon public bodies. However, we would like to continue to apply sustainable development duties on new bodies as they are created as

---

[2] Information about the National School of Government can be found at www.nationalschool.gov.uk
[3] see the sustainable development website at www.sustainable-development.gov.uk

appropriate to their role and remit, and to assess whether a specific sustainable development duty should be applied to existing key bodies in priority areas. The important issue is whether a new duty would promote better delivery of sustainable development.

3. Strengthening regional delivery

Taking it on consultation responses

Respondents endorsed the 'Taking it on' priorities, but pointed out that those national policies were not responsive enough to regional differences – such as the need for solutions for a growing and ageing population in the South West, overheating in the South East, housing growth in the East of England and tackling the differing needs for urban and rural communities in the West Midlands.

Respondents felt that regional sustainable development frameworks (rsdfs) currently lacked authority. This made delivery difficult – for example, in some places, other regional strategies are not consistent with rsdfs.

The general consensus was that indicators are currently not sufficiently outcome-focused, consistent and flexible to enable regions to assess their performance against the national situation.

One of the big changes since 1999 has been the increased devolution of responsibility for strategic direction to regional levels. A key task will be to strengthen regional leadership.

Regional Development Agencies (RDAs) have been set up by Government to transform England's regions through sustainable economic development and to have an influential role in the business community. The RDAs, which have a statutory duty to contribute to sustainable development in the UK, prepare and implement Regional Economic Strategies (RES). The new Tasking Framework for RDA corporate plans for 2005-2008 supports RDAs in mainstreaming sustainable development in all of their programmes.

> ❯ **The Government will update guidance on preparing Regional Economic Strategies in 2005 to help RDAs in delivering economic growth and sustainable development**

Regional Assemblies scrutinise the work of their RDA and have been appointed as the regional planning body with a duty to prepare the statutory Regional Spatial Strategies (RSS). They also play a leading role in work on integrating regional strategies and drawing up rsdfs with key players and a wide range of regional expert groups and stakeholders. These high level frameworks set out objectives and priorities for sustainable development in the region and inform regional strategies, including those developed by the RDAs, and the RSS, as well as sub-regional strategies, including Sustainable Community Strategies. In several regions rsdfs take the form of an Integrated Regional Strategy.

Research on regional sustainable development frameworks

The English Regions Network[4] found that the rsdf process requires organisations to work together and get to grips with each other's viewpoint. This raises issues about expertise and understanding of regional sustainable development among the participants. Stakeholders cited examples of how their work on rsdfs had influenced their work on other strategies. While the study could not firmly attribute particular changes in particular plans and strategies to rsdfs, it did see a greater recognition of sustainable development in other strategies.

The study recommended that future rsdfs should have:

> more structured and representative stakeholder involvement

> better defined and prioritised objectives and associated targets

> action plans that

  – address unsustainable activity at the regional level

  – set out responsibilities and tasks against defined time-scales, and

> more effective monitoring processes.

[4] Research into regional sustainable development frameworks. Final report to the English Regions Network by CAG consultants and Oxford Brookes University School of Planning.

Responses to the consultation confirmed the findings of the English Regions Network research. They identified the need for a framework for sustainable development in each region with certain core elements developed in consultation with regional stakeholders. This framework should set out:

❯ a shared vision for the region

❯ objectives, priorities and targets for advancing sustainable development

❯ action plans showing which organisations will be responsible for delivering on each of the agreed priorities

❯ a range of indicators relevant to the region and regional issues. Measuring and reporting, where data is available, on performance at regional level on indicators linked to the UK Framework Indicators will be particularly useful in showing how regional activity can contribute to sustainable development at the national level, and

❯ arrangements for monitoring and review.

❯ **The Government will produce up-dated guidance on rsdfs, reflecting this new UK Strategy and including a clarification of the role of the Regional Assemblies, pending the outcome of a review (see below)**

Inter-regional growth strategies, such as the 'Northern Way'[5], 'Smart Growth: The Midlands Way', and 'The Way Ahead: The South West Way' are seeking to promote greater inter-regional collaboration, with a particular emphasis on the Regional Economic Strategy (RES), economic development priorities, land use and natural resources, in ways that allow this to be translated to the respective Regional Spatial Strategies (RSSs) across adjoining regions. The Government is exploring how to provide a stronger and more consistent economic evidence base and methodology to underpin both the RES and the RSS. The Government is:

❯ **considering the responses to consultation on proposals to merge the regional planning body role of Regional Assemblies with the role of Regional Housing Boards**

❯ **examining ways to achieve more integration of regional transport, economic development and housing programmes within a framework of long-term regional funding allocations**

❯ **developing a methodology which will allow a national view to be taken on the relationship between regions on key issues including the consequences of alternative economic scenarios as a result of migration, household numbers, the impact of housing supply and house prices, and**

❯ **undertaking research to provide a clearer economic and demographic context for regional planning over the next 25 years. This will explore regional disparities and inter-regional relationships and how these relate to each other and the wider economy**

---

[5] For more details go to www.odpm.gov.uk

Government Offices (GOs) represent central Government departments in the regions. They work with regional partners to ensure the joined-up delivery of the policies of ODPM, DTI, Defra, DfES, HO, DfT, CO, DCMS and DWP. All of these contribute to sustainable development as set out in this strategy. This is reflected in GO Business Plans and evidence from GOs on regional performance will demonstrate their contribution to sustainable development. Regional Directors of Public Health and their teams work with the Government Office to ensure that the public health dimensions of sustainable development are promoted and considered across a range of different policy areas. They will also work with Strategic Health Authorities to encourage the links between rsdfs and the NHS, so the Health Service is working within the context of sustainable development.

Bodies such as the new Integrated Agency and the Environment Agency (see Chapter 5) also have a strong regional presence and contribute to delivering sustainable development at regional level.

The Government will continue to engage regional stakeholders in policy development in line with the joint Cabinet Office/ODPM guidance 'Incorporating regional perspectives into the policy making process'.

> ▶ **The Government will continue to explore ways to increase cross departmental 'joined-up working' with key regional stakeholders on national policy development and will hold workshops with key stakeholders**

> ▶ **The Government will also look for new ways to help regions contribute fully to sustainable development, as measured by the UK Government Strategy Indicators and any regionally selected indicators**

> ▶ **The Sustainable Development Commission will review the overall arrangements for delivering sustainable development in the regions – including rsdfs, regional sustainable development networks, liaison between central Government and the regions, and the role of major regional bodies and strategies – and make recommendations for improving effectiveness**

4. Strengthening local delivery

Local authorities and their partners, through Local Strategic Partnerships, are pivotal to delivering sustainable communities.

Taking it on consultation responses

The 'Taking it on' consultation indicated that the new joined-up processes being developed for local Government and local service providers, were well placed to contribute to development of sustainable development, through strong local leadership and better partnership working, if central Government could link these to work on sustainable communities, planning and regeneration.

Making the vision of sustainable communities a reality at the local level means sending the right signals to local Government about the importance of sustainable development, supporting strong local leadership and developing the right skills and knowledge.

Working with the Local Government Association, the Improvement and Development Agency, the Audit Commission and other stakeholders through the Central Local Partnership, the Government has developed an action plan which will ensure delivery of sustainable development at the local level. This action plan will also help support implementation of our proposals for empowering community action on sustainable development through Community Action 2020 – Together We Can in Chapter 2 and the creation of sustainable communities in Chapter 6 and is in line with the developing ten-year strategy for local Government.

From 2005, the Central Local Partnership will receive an annual progress report on the delivery of the action plan set out below.

Sending the right signals

> **In 2005 the Government will hold a cross-departmental workshop to explore ways of improving the Government's communication of consistent messages on sustainable development and sustainable communities to local Government.**

> **The Comprehensive Performance Assessment (CPA) process from 2005 onwards, including the Key Lines of Enquiry and Guidance to Inspectors, will seek to recognise and reward good performance on sustainable development and community engagement. We will work with the Audit Commission to train CPA Inspectors and equip them with a good understanding of sustainable development as a whole and how it applies to the CPA process.**

> **The next rounds of Beacon Council Themes (rounds 7 and 8) will include themes around aspects of sustainable development at the local level.**

Making best use of existing tools to support local leadership

> **During 2005 the Government will work with its partners to develop toolkits and other materials to support Local Strategic Partnerships (LSPs) in developing and delivering Sustainable Community Strategies which help deliver sustainable development in the UK.**

> **During 2005 the Government, Local Government Association and IDeA will develop a joint central-local government commitment to the delivery of sustainable development in the context of the new vision on sustainable communities. This commitment will harness the energies of local authorities and their partners and will allow freedom and flexibility in the approach taken at the local level.**

Skills and knowledge for local public sector bodies

> **Following the recommendation contained in Sir John Egan's Review 'Skills for Sustainable Communities' (2004), the Government has announced the establishment of a new Academy for Sustainable Communities. The Academy will work with partners to promote a new agenda for sustainable communities, increase the availability of generic skills and widen and improve access to sustainable communities skills. The Academy's programme will include the development of learning opportunities for the core occupations identified in the Egan Review, including those for Local Strategic Partnerships.**

▶ **On the theme of 'cleaner, safer, greener communities' the Government will launch a 'How To' programme to promote the take up and use of new and existing powers and guidance to transform the local environment. The Government will also provide a joined up programme of support for our delivery partners to promote the improvement of the local environment.**

▶ **The Improvement and Development Agency will roll out a Leadership Academy module on Sustainable Communities which develops local leadership on sustainable development issues. It will also offer a peer review tool on 'Sustainable Communities'.**

▶ **In addition, the Government will improve local Government skills and knowledge on sustainable communities through wider training schemes such as the Local Government Capacity Building Programme.**

The Government has established nine Regional Centres of Excellence (RCEs) across England – one in each region. ODPM is responsible for implementing the system for measuring efficiency gains made by local authorities and it also sponsors the RCEs. The RCEs are the lead change agents for local Government, assisting councils in finding and making efficiency gains. The RCEs are also responsible for taking forward the actions of the National Procurement Strategy for Local Government adopted in 2004 by ODPM and the Local Government Association.

During 2005, we will work through the RCEs to encourage sustainable procurement throughout local Government and improved skills training.

The Government will:

▶ **ask the RCEs to champion a number of sustainable procurement themes including sustainable energy, sustainable waste, sustainable food, sustainable timber and minimum product standards, and**

▶ **disseminate good practice to local authorities and other Regional Centres in order to build skills, knowledge and understanding on sustainable procurement: in particular, that produced by the European Procura Plus sustainable procurement campaign[6].**

5. International delivery

The world needs more effective ways to deliver international sustainable development. The Foreign Office (FCO), Defra, DFID, DTI and HMT share responsibility for helping deliver international development that is more sustainable. This is co-ordinated by the Interdepartmental Working Group on International Sustainable Development that will ensure that we are delivering on our commitments and co-ordinate progress reporting to Ministers, Parliament, and the public.

The FCO has developed its own sustainable development strategy to be published in March 2005. This will set out how the FCO will help deliver the UK's international priorities on sustainable development, focusing on those areas where the FCO adds value to the implementation of this strategy. Where appropriate in international delivery

[6] See www.iclei-europe.org/index.php?procuraplus>

work, Government departments will draw on the expertise of other public bodies. For example, the Environment Agency is providing technical advice and practical support on matters such as water management, environmental governance, regulation and enforcement.

As Chapter 6 states, the Department for International Development (DFID) manages the UK's Overseas Development Assistance. The Department's work is defined by the International Development Act (2002), which requires development funds to be used for poverty reduction, either through furthering sustainable development or improving the welfare of a population[7]. Poverty reduction and sustainable development go hand in hand. The Millennium Development Goals (MDGs), agreed by the international community in 2000, define the key objectives for reducing poverty and encouraging development in poor countries. DFID has made the MDGs the main focus of its work.

The UK's international network of diplomatic representatives and development officers, including the FCO's environment attachés and science attachés network and DFID country staff, will play a significant role in delivering and explaining the UK's international priorities. The environment attachés are supported by **epnet**, a website for Government officials working on environment issues which provides an international network. It aims to keep staff in overseas posts, particularly the environment attachés, up to date with policy and to give them the information they need to deliver UK priorities.

Epnet is being redeveloped and will be re-launched in 2005 as a sustainable development network in order to better support environment attachés in leading on delivering sustainable development through this strategy and to reflect the wide range of issues that they work on.

> **From April 2005 there will be a new programme, as part of the FCO's Global Opportunities Fund, called the Sustainable Development Programme.**

The programme will fund projects in priority countries, focusing on the following themes:

> transparency, information, participation and access to justice (including freedom of expression, environmental democracy and rule of law)

> core human rights priorities (including combating torture, abolishing the death penalty and promoting children's rights), and

> natural resource management (including sustainable forest management and reduction of illegal logging, biodiversity and sustainable tourism).

This will be complemented by additional Defra funding to help deliver commitments from the World Summit on Sustainable Development (WSSD).

Departments will work with a number of rapidly developing countries on integrating principles of sustainable development into country policies and programmes, and implementing action plans in support of these in line with MDG 7 and WSSD's 2005 target for national strategies.

---

[7] Funds may also be used to support British Overseas Territories and for humanitarian assistance.

> **Bilateral Sustainable Development Dialogues will be established with China and India. Agreed at Prime Ministerial level these dialogues will build on, and provide a framework for, existing country-level activities as well as identify new areas of collaboration. It is envisaged that this will involve mutual learning on how both countries approach sustainable development planning and delivery, looking at institutional capacity and co-ordination, underpinned by specific joint projects in a range of policy areas.**

We shall continue to use our Environment for Europe Fund (EfE) to support small environmental projects in the candidate countries for the European Union and Eastern Europe, Caucasus & Central Asia (EECCA) countries. At a higher level, we shall press for EU funding to be used judiciously to support the delivery of WSSD and EfE commitments, and the MDGs.

The Overseas Territories Environment Programme, jointly funded by the FCO and DFID, will continue to support implementation of Environment Charters in the Territories.

In addition, partnerships between Government and civil society groups including NGOs and business are an important means of delivering action on the ground, developing new ideas and innovative solutions. The UK's priority is to make partnership working a significant means of implementation through:

> embedding partnership working in the UN CSD work programme

> maintaining the voluntary, self-organising nature of partnerships, while fostering transparency and accountability

> encouraging the exchange of good practice and experience

> providing start-up funding for new partnerships, and

> working to break down policy barriers to partnership activity.

The Government has compiled a table of the UK's international priorities for sustainable development primarily arising from WSSD, Doha, Monterrey and the MDGs. This includes aims, lead departments, and sources of information. The table can be found at the end of this chapter and will also be published on the Government's sustainable development website as a live document. It will be developed and updated as the Strategy is implemented and used as a monitoring and reporting tool.

The UK Government works within the United Nations system and with international financial institutions to promote a co-ordinated approach to environmental, social and economic issues.

At the 2005 UN Millennium Review Summit the UK Government will aim to promote increased international effort to achieve the MDGs and related commitments including those from WSSD focussing particularly on climate change, water and sanitation and environmental sustainability.

Under its new work programme the UN Commission on Sustainable Development addresses sustainable development commitments over seven two-year cycles with each cycle focusing on a thematic cluster of issues. The cycle is divided into a "review year" and a "policy year". We aim to ensure that each two-year cycle agrees policy responses and concrete actions to tackle the problems identified in the review year.

We continue to work with other states on strengthening the United Nations Environment Programme (UNEP), which is mandated to promote the environmental dimension across the UN system.

In particular we want to see:

> greater and more predictable financing for the Programme

> effective implementation of the Bali Strategic Plan for Technology Support and Capacity Building in environmental matters, and

> enhanced co-ordination across the UN system, especially between UNEP and the UN Development Programme.

The UK is playing an active role in discussions on strengthening international environmental governance, such as the proposals for UNEP to be transferred into a UN specialised agency.

6. How to know if this strategy has been successful

Government departments and their executive agencies will produce Action Plans setting out how they intend to implement the commitments in this strategy and will report progress against these, for example in their annual departmental reports.

The Government will monitor the policy commitments and the indicators set out in each of the chapters in the Strategy (summarised at the end of this chapter), and the relevant Public Service Agreement (PSA) targets. We will take action if evidence from monitoring and evaluation, including latest information on these indicators, shows that we are not likely to meet targets, or deliver the policy commitments.

The Sustainable Development Programme Board will use this information to ensure that the Strategy is delivered and commitments met, supported by Defra's Sustainable Development Unit as its secretariat.

As part of this commitment to monitor progress, quarterly reports will be made to HM Treasury on performance on PSA targets, including Defra's overarching target on sustainable development.

Government Offices will report progress at regional and sub-regional levels through new performance monitoring arrangements and Regional Development Agencies will be accountable for progress through the new Tasking Framework. Local Authorities will be monitored through Comprehensive Performance Assessment.

The Government will monitor and report annually on the UK Framework Indicators to place the Government's performance in context. This report will form the basis of the UK's reporting to the UN Commission on Sustainable Development which monitors progress internationally.

The Office of National Statistics[8] will continue to produce a set of national satellite accounts annually, which take into account a range of uncosted factors, for example environmental impacts.

---

[8] Available at www.sustainable.gov.uk

Up to now, progress against our national strategy has only been provided in reports drawn up by Government itself. We believe that we should now move to independent scrutiny of action on sustainable development across Government to determine whether real progress is being made. That will not be achieved by Government reporting on itself. **So we propose that the strengthened Sustainable Development Commission (SDC) should act as a "watchdog" for sustainable development.** It will provide assurance and will report on progress towards implementing the UK Framework and the commitments in the UK Government Strategy, including on the institutional and accountability arrangements, as well as focusing in more depth on particular issues.

To have maximum impact the SDC will need to work with the House of Common's Environmental Audit Committee and the National Audit Office. The Environmental Audit Committee, which reports to Parliament, has an important role in scrutinising and reporting on Government's performance on sustainable development. It has the ability to call Departments to give evidence on sustainable development. The Committee has recently been supported by the expertise of the National Audit Office which has been expanding the time and effort it spends on these issues.

Our integrated approach for ensuring it happens

- National School for Government
- Academy for Sustainable Communities
- Regional Centres of Excellence
- Revised guidance for bodies with SD duties
- Enhanced SDC advisory function
- IDeA leadership Academy SD module

Enable

Encourage

- SDC watchdog function
- Beacon Councils
- Performance management systems, eg CPA
- International SD programme
- Indicators and targets

Engage

- SD Programme Board
- SD Task Force
- SD dialogues with overseas stakeholders
- Support for Local Strategic Partnerships

Exemplify

- SD Action Plans
- SD duty on new bodies where appropriate
- Best practice RIAs
- Regional SD Frameworks
- Framework for SD in Govt estate review

7. Measuring our progress overall

The full list of indicators to be used to monitor progress in the UK Government Strategy is set out below, along with Public Service Agreements and other policy objectives which will most directly contribute to progress. All the UK Framework Indicators are included and are indicated by an asterisk.

A very large number of indicators are used across Government to monitor the outcomes of policies. There is an even larger number if those used by other organisations and internationally are considered. The vast majority of these indicators are or have the potential to be covering issues pertinent to sustainable development. Experience from the 1999 Strategy suggested that although there was some merit in having a large set of indicators – in the 1999 Strategy there were 147 – in practice it was difficult to determine overall progress and the majority of indicators were also monitored elsewhere. On the other hand the 15 headline indicators in the 1999 Strategy were used extensively in reporting progress, but could only provide a broad overview.

For the UK Government Strategy, we have established a set of 68 indicators, consisting of the 20 UK Framework Indicators and a further 48 indicators with which to monitor progress.

In trying to establish a set of indicators to support the UK Government Strategy, we have attempted to focus on the key priorities for sustainable development. Nevertheless, there may be issues that some people think are not adequately covered by the indicators. If in due course there is a strong case for some additional indicators then, where practicable, we will of course introduce new indicators. By the same token, if it becomes apparent that certain indicators need to be improved to ensure our monitoring is effective then if it is practicable to establish a revised indicator, we will do so. However it should be noted that there are considerable economic, statistical, scientific, and practical constraints to embarking on new data collection.

The indicators selected here to support the UK Government Strategy have been chosen as key measures of impacts or drivers for priorities within the Strategy. As far as practicable we have taken into account comments and suggestions on indicators received in response to the 'Taking it on' consultation. Some of the indicators were previously established to underpin and monitor the 1999 Strategy and are considered appropriate to continue with, others have been newly developed, such as 'decoupling' indicators for sustainable consumption and production. We have also considered indicators used for other purposes across Government, by the Devolved Administrations, and where practicable internationally. We are constrained by the availability of existing data sources or established indicators, but some issues we consider to be sufficiently important that we have highlighted the need for a new indicator to be developed.

> **A separate statistical report providing the baseline figures for our indicators will be published in June 2005**

At the same time, where possible, the Government will outline the work to be undertaken to establish the indicators for which we currently do not have data. Additionally, on the UK Government sustainable development website, we intend to provide links to a wide range of international indicators, so that people can assess the UK's progress internationally and have access to information on global trends.

Conclusion

This strategy is the result of wide-spread, inclusive consultation and a very high degree of co-operation between a range of Government and other public sector bodies.

The challenge is now to implement this to ensure that sustainable development is delivered on the ground – securing the future for all of us.

UK GOVERNMENT STRATEGY INDICATORS	Related Public Service Agreements (PSA) and other relevant policy statements
1. **Greenhouse gas emissions***: Kyoto target and CO_2 emissions	**Defra PSA 2, DTI PSA 4, DfT PSA 8** To reduce greenhouse gas emissions to 12.5% below 1990 levels in line with our Kyoto commitment and move towards a 20% reduction in carbon dioxide emissions below 1990 levels by 2010, through measures including energy efficiency and renewables
2. **CO_2 emissions by end user:** industry, domestic, transport (excluding international aviation), other	
3. **Aviation and shipping emissions:** greenhouse gases from UK-based international aviation and shipping fuel bunkers	**DfT White Papers:** 'The Future of Air Transport' and 'British shipping: Charting a new course'
4. **Renewable electricity:** renewable electricity generated as a percentage of total electricity	**Defra PSA 2, DTI PSA 4** To reduce greenhouse gas emissions to 12.5% below 1990 levels in line with our Kyoto commitment and move towards a 20% reduction in carbon dioxide emissions below 1990 levels by 2010, through measures including energy efficiency and renewables
5. **Electricity generation:** electricity generated, CO_2, NO_x and SO_2 emissions by electricity generators and GDP	
6. **Household energy use:** domestic CO_2 emissions and household final consumption expenditure	**DTI White Paper:** "Our energy future – creating a low carbon economy"
7. **Road transport:** CO_2, NO_x, PM_{10} emissions and GDP	**DfT PSA 6, Defra PSA 8** Improve air quality by meeting the Air Quality Strategy targets for carbon monoxide, lead, nitrogen dioxide, particles, sulphur dioxide, benzene and 1,3 butadiene **DfT PSA 7, Defra PSA 2, DTI PSA 4** To reduce greenhouse gas emissions to 12.5% below 1990 levels in line with our Kyoto commitment and move towards a 20% reduction in carbon dioxide emissions below 1990 levels by 2010, through measures including energy efficiency and renewables
8. **Private vehicles:** CO_2 emissions and car-km and household final consumption expenditure	
9. **Road freight:** CO_2 emissions and tonne-km, tonnes and GDP	
10. **Manufacturing sector:** CO_2, NO_x, SO_2, PM_{10} emissions and GVA	**DTI:** 'The Government's Manufacturing Strategy' and 'Competing In the Global Economy: The Government's Manufacturing Strategy Two Years On'
11. **Service sector:** CO_2, NO_x emissions and GVA	
12. **Public sector:** CO_2, NO_x emissions and GVA	Sustainable Development in Government Framework
13. **Resource use*:** Domestic Material Consumption and GDP	**Defra, DTI:** Changing Patterns: UK Government Framework for Sustainable Consumption and Production
14. **Energy supply:** UK primary energy supply and gross inland energy consumption	**DTI PSA 4** Lead work to deliver the goals of energy policy: maintain the reliability of energy supplies

UK GOVERNMENT STRATEGY INDICATORS	Related Public Service Agreements (PSA) and other relevant policy statements
15. Water resource use: total abstractions from non-tidal surface and ground water sources and GDP	**Defra and Environment Agency** Water Framework Directive **Defra** Water Strategy: 'Directing the Flow – priorities for future water policy'
16. Domestic water consumption: domestic water consumption per head	
17. Water stress: *(to be developed to monitor the impacts of water shortages)*	
18. Waste*: arisings by (a) sector (b) method of disposal	**Defra PSA 6** Enable at least 25% of household waste to be recycled or composted by 2005-06, with further improvements by 2008
19. Household waste: (a) arisings (b) recycled or composted	
20. Bird populations*: bird population indices (a) farmland birds* (b) woodland birds* (c) birds of coasts and estuaries* (d) wintering wetland birds	**Defra PSA 3** Care for our natural heritage, make the countryside attractive and enjoyable for all and preserve biological diversity by: ➤ reversing the long-term decline in the number of farmland birds by 2020, as measured annually against underlying trends
21. Biodiversity conservation: (a) priority species status (b) priority habitat status	**Defra PSA 3** Care for our natural heritage, make the countryside attractive and enjoyable for all and preserve biological diversity by: ➤ reversing the long-term decline in the number of farmland birds by 2020, as measured annually against underlying trends; and ➤ bringing into favourable condition, by 2010, 95% of all nationally important wildlife sites
22. Agriculture sector: fertiliser input, farmland bird population, and ammonia and methane emissions and output	**Defra PSA 5** Deliver more customer-focused, competitive and sustainable farming and food industries and secure further progress, via Common Agricultural Policy (CAP) and World Trade Organisation (WTO) negotiations, in reducing CAP trade-distorting support **Defra:** "Strategy for Sustainable Farming and Food: Facing the Future"
23. Farming and environmental stewardship: *(to be developed to monitor progress in new stewardship schemes)*	
24. Land use: area used for agriculture, woodland, water or river, urban (contextual indicator)	
25. Land recycling: (a) new dwellings built on previously developed land or through conversions (b) all new development on previously developed land	**ODPM PSA 6** The planning system to deliver sustainable development outcomes at national, regional and local levels through efficient and high quality planning and development management processes, including through achievement of best value standards for planning by 2008
26. Dwelling density: average density of new housing	
27. Fish stocks*: fish stocks around the UK within sustainable limits	**Defra** Sustainable Fisheries Programme

UK GOVERNMENT STRATEGY INDICATORS	Related Public Service Agreements (PSA) and other relevant policy statements
28. Ecological impacts of air pollution*: area of UK habitat sensitive to acidification and eutrophication with critical load exceedences	**DfT PSA 6, Defra PSA 8** Improve air quality by meeting the Air Quality Strategy targets for carbon monoxide, lead, nitrogen dioxide, particles, sulphur dioxide, benzene and 1,3 butadiene
29. Emissions of air pollutants: SO_2, NO_x, NH_3 and PM_{10} emissions and GDP	
30. River quality*: rivers of good (a) biological (b) chemical quality	**Defra and Environment Agency** Improved river water quality, as measured by compliance with River Quality Objectives
31. Flooding: (*to be developed to monitor sustainable approaches to ongoing flood management*)	**Defra and Environment Agency** Sustainable policies for river and coastal flood management evidenced by implementation of 'Making Space for Water' strategy and completion of strategic Catchment Flood Management and Shoreline Management Plans
32. Economic output*: Gross Domestic Product	**HMT PSA 1** Demonstrate by 2008 progress on the Government's long-term objective of raising the trend rate of growth over the economic cycle by at least meeting the Budget 2004 projection
33. Productivity: UK output per worker	**HMT PSA 1** Demonstrate by 2008 progress on the Government's long-term objective of raising the trend rate of growth over the economic cycle by at least meeting the Budget 2004 projection

DTI PSA 1, HMT PSA 4 Demonstrate further progress by 2008 on the Government's long-term objective of raising the rate of UK productivity growth over the economic cycle, improving competitiveness and narrowing the gap with our major industrial competitors

DTI PSA 6 Build an enterprise society in which small firms of all kinds thrive and achieve their potential, with an improvement in the overall productivity of small firms

Defra PSA 4 Reduce the gap in productivity between the least well performing quartile of rural areas and the English median by 2008, demonstrating progress by 2006, and improve the accessibility of services for people in rural areas

DCMS PSA 4 By 2008, improve the productivity of the tourism, creative and leisure industries |

UK GOVERNMENT STRATEGY INDICATORS	Related Public Service Agreements (PSA) and other relevant policy statements
34. Investment: (a) total investment (b) social investment relative to GDP	**HM Treasury:** Budget 2004
35. Demography: population and population of working age (contextual indicator)	
36. Households and dwellings: households, single person households and dwelling stock (contextual indicator)	**ODPM:** 'Housing Policy Statement, The Way Forward for Housing' **ODPM PSA 5** Achieve a better balance between housing availability and the demand for housing, including improving affordability, in all English regions while protecting valuable countryside around our towns, cities and in the green belt and the sustainability of towns and cities.
37. Active community participation*: informal and formal volunteering at least once a month	**Home Office PSA 6** Increase voluntary and community engagement, especially amongst those at risk of social exclusion. **Home Office PSA 7** Reduce race inequalities and build community cohesion.
38. Crime*: crime survey and recorded crime for (a) vehicles (b) domestic burglary (c) violence	**Home Office PSA 1** Reduce crime by 15%, and further in high crime areas, by 2007-08. Target contributing to the Criminal Justice System PSA (PSA 1).
39. Fear of crime: (a) car theft (b) burglary (c) physical attack	**Home Office PSA 2, DCA PSA 2, CPS PSA 2** Reassure the public, reducing the fear of crime and anti-social behaviour, and building confidence in the Criminal Justice System without compromising fairness. Target contributing to the Criminal Justice System PSA (PSA 3).
40. Employment*: people of working age in employment **41. Workless households*:** population living in workless households (a) children (b) working age	**DWP PSA 4, HMT PSA 5** As part of the wider objective of full employment in every region, over the three years to Spring 2008, and taking account of the economic cycle: ‣ demonstrate progress on increasing the employment rate ‣ increase the employment rates of disadvantaged groups (lone parents, ethnic minorities, people aged 50 and over, those with the lowest qualifications and those living in the local authority wards with the poorest initial labour market position); and ‣ significantly reduce the difference between the employment rates of the disadvantaged groups and the overall rate.

UK GOVERNMENT STRATEGY INDICATORS	Related Public Service Agreements (PSA) and other relevant policy statements
42. Economically inactive: people of working age who are economically inactive	**DWP PSA 1, HMT PSA 7** Halve the number of children in relative low-income households between 1998-99 and 2010-11, on the way to eradicating child poverty by 2020 including:
43. Childhood poverty*: children in relative low-income households a) before housing costs b) after housing costs	‣ reducing the proportion of children living in workless households by 5% between spring 2005 and spring 2008; and ‣ increasing the proportion of Parents with Care on Income Support and income-based Jobseeker's Allowance who receive maintenance for their children to 65% by March 2008. (The Government will also set a target as part of the next Spending Review to halve by 2010-11 the numbers of children suffering a combination of material deprivation and relative low income. The target will be met if there is an equivalent proportional reduction to that required on relative low income between 2004-05 and 2010-11) **DWP PSA 3, DfES PSA 2** As a contribution to reducing the proportion of children living in households where no-one is working, by 2008: ‣ increase the stock of Ofsted-registered childcare by 10%; ‣ increase the take-up of formal childcare by lower income families by 50%; and ‣ introduce by April 2005, a successful light-touch childcare approval scheme. Sure Start Unit target
44. Young adults: 16-19 year-olds not in employment, education or training	**DfES PSA 12** Reduce the proportion of young people not in education, employment or training by 2 percentage points by 2010
45. Pensioner poverty*: pensioners in relative low-income households a) before housing costs b) after housing costs	**DWP PSA 6** By 2008, be paying Pension Credit to at least 3.2 million pensioner households, while maintaining a focus on the most disadvantaged by ensuring that at least 2.2 million of these households are in receipt of the Guarantee Credit
46. Pension provision: working age people contributing to a non-state pension in at least three years out of the last four	**DH PSA 8** Improve the quality of life and independence of vulnerable older people by supporting them to live in their own homes where possible by: ‣ increasing the proportion of older people being supported to live in their own home by 1% annually in 2007 and 2008; and ‣ increasing by 2008, the proportion of those supported intensively to live at home to 34% of the total of those being supported at home or in residential care **Defra PSA 7, DTI PSA 4** Eliminate fuel poverty in vulnerable households in England by 2010 in line with the Government's Fuel Poverty Strategy objective

UK GOVERNMENT STRATEGY INDICATORS	Related Public Service Agreements (PSA) and other relevant policy statements
47. Education*: 19 year-olds with level 2 qualifications and above	**DfES PSA 11** Increase the proportion of 19 year olds who achieve at least level 2 by 3 percentage points between 2004 and 2006, and a further 2 percentage points between 2006 and 2008, and increase the proportion of young people who achieve level 3
48. Sustainable development education: *(to be developed to monitor the impact of formal learning on knowledge and awareness of sustainable development)*	
49. Health inequality*: (a) infant mortality (by socio-economic group) (b) life expectancy (by area) for men and women	**DH PSA 2** Reduce health inequalities by 10% by 2010 as measured by infant mortality and life expectancy at birth
50. Healthy life expectancy: healthy life expectancy (a) men (b) women	
51. Mortality rates: death rates from (a) circulatory disease and (b) cancer, below 75 years and for areas with the worst health and deprivation indicators, and (c) suicides	**DH PSA 1** Substantially reduce mortality rates by 2010: ▸ from heart disease and stroke and related diseases by at least 40% in people under 75, with at least a 40% reduction in the inequalities gap between the fifth of areas with the worst health and deprivation indicators and the population as a whole; ▸ from cancer by at least 20% in people under 75, with a reduction in the inequalities gap of at least 6% between the fifth of areas with the worst health and deprivation indicators and the population as a whole; and ▸ from suicide and undetermined injury by at least 20%
52. Smoking: prevalence of smoking (a) all adults (b) 'routine and manual' socio-economic groups	**DH PSA 3** Tackle the underlying determinants of ill health and health inequalities by: ▸ reducing adult smoking rates to 21% or less by 2010, with a reduction in prevalence among routine and manual groups to 26% or less
53. Childhood obesity: prevalence of obesity in 2-10 year-olds	**DH PSA 3, DfES PSA 4, DCMS PSA 2** Tackle the underlying determinants of ill health and health inequalities by: ▸ halting the year-on-year rise in obesity among children under 11 by 2010 in the context of a broader strategy to tackle obesity in the population as a whole
54. Diet: people consuming five or more portions of fruit and vegetables per day and in low income households	**DH:** 'Food and Health Action Plan'

UK GOVERNMENT STRATEGY INDICATORS	Related Public Service Agreements (PSA) and other relevant policy statements
55. Mobility*: (a) number of trips per person by mode (b) distance travelled per person per year by broad trip purpose	**DfT PSA 3** By 2010, increase the use of public transport (bus and light rail) by more than 12% in England compared with 2000 levels, with growth in every region
56. Getting to school: how children get to school	**DfT:** 'Walking and cycling: an action plan'
57. Accessibility: access to key services	**ODPM PSA 4** By 2008, improve the effectiveness and efficiency of local government in leading and delivering services to all communities **Defra PSA 4** Improve the accessibility of services for people in rural areas
58. Road accidents: number of people and children killed or seriously injured	**DfT PSA 5** Reduce the number of people killed or seriously injured in Great Britain in road accidents by 40% and the number of children killed or seriously injured by 50%, by 2010 compared with the average for 1994-98, tackling the significantly higher incidence in disadvantaged communities
59. Social justice*: (social measures to be developed)	**ODPM PSA 1** Tackle social exclusion and deliver neighbourhood renewal, working with departments to help them meet their PSA floor targets, in particular narrowing the gap in health, education, crime, worklessness, housing and liveability outcomes between the most deprived areas and the rest of England, with measurable improvement by 2010
60. Environmental equality*: (environmental measures to be developed)	**ODPM PSA 8** Lead the delivery of cleaner, safer and greener public spaces and improvement of the quality of the built environment in deprived areas and across the country, with measurable improvement by 2008
61. Air quality and health: (a) annual levels of particles and ozone (b) days when air pollution is moderate or higher	**DfT PSA 6, Defra PSA 8** Improve air quality by meeting the Air Quality Strategy targets for carbon monoxide, lead, nitrogen dioxide, particles, sulphur dioxide, benzene and 1,3 butadiene
62. Housing conditions: (a) social sector homes below the decent homes standard (b) vulnerable households in the private sector in homes below the decent homes standard	**ODPM PSA 7** By 2010, bring all social housing into a decent condition with most of this improvement taking place in deprived areas, and for vulnerable households in the private sector, including families with children, increase the proportion who live in homes that are in decent condition
63. Households living in fuel poverty: (a) pensioners (b) households with children (c) disabled/long-term sick	**Defra PSA 7, DTI PSA 3** Eliminate fuel poverty in vulnerable households in England by 2010 in line with the Government's Fuel Poverty Strategy objective

UK GOVERNMENT STRATEGY INDICATORS	Related Public Service Agreements (PSA) and other relevant policy statements
64. Homelessness: (a) rough sleepers (b) households in temporary accommodation (i) total (ii) households with children	**ODPM:** "Sustainable Communities: Homes for all" **ODPM PSA 1** Tackle social exclusion and deliver neighbourhood renewal, working with Departments to help them meet their PSA floor targets, in particular narrowing the gap in health, education, crime, worklessness, housing and liveability outcomes between the most deprived areas and the rest of England, with measurable improvements by 2010 **ODPM PSA 4** By 2008, improve the effectiveness and efficiency of local government in leading and delivery services to all communities **ODPM PSA 5** Achieve a better balance between housing availability and the demand for housing, including improving affordability, in all English regions while protecting valuable countryside around our towns, cities and in the green belt and the sustainability of towns and cities
65. Local environment quality: *(to be developed using information from the Local Environmental Quality Survey of England)*	**ODPM PSA 8** Lead the delivery of cleaner, safer and greener public spaces and improvement of the quality of the built environment in deprived areas and across the country, with measurable improvement by 2008
66. Satisfaction in local area: households satisfied with the quality of the places in which they live (a) overall (b) in deprived areas (c) non-decent homes	**ODPM PSA 8** Lead the delivery of cleaner, safer and greener public spaces and improvement of the quality of the built environment in deprived areas and across the country, with measurable improvement by 2008
67. UK International assistance: Net Official Development Assistance (a) per cent of Gross National Income (comparison with selected countries) (b) per capita (comparison with selected countries)	**DfID PSA 3** Improved effectiveness of the multilateral system, as demonstrated by: ▸ a greater impact of EC external programmes on poverty reduction and working for agreement to increase the proportion of EC official development assistance (ODA) to low income countries from its 2000 baseline figure of 38% to 70% by 2008; ▸ ensuring that 90% of all eligible Heavily Indebted Poor Countries committed to poverty reduction that have reached Decision Point by end 2005, receive irrevocable debt relief by end 2008. Joint with HMT PSA 8 ▸ international partners working effectively with poor countries to make progress towards the United Nations 2015 Millennium Development Goals, joint with HM Treasury; and ▸ improved effectiveness of United Nations agencies and the humanitarian aid system
68. Wellbeing*: *(wellbeing measures to be developed)*	

* An indicator within the UK's shared framework for sustainable development 'One future – different paths'

Public Service Agreements are for 2005-2008 within the 2004 Spending Review
GDP, Gross Domestic Product, a measure of national economic output
GVA, Gross Value Added, a measure of sectoral economic output
CO_2, Carbon dioxide, a greenhouse gas and the main contributor to global warming
NO_x, Nitrogen oxides, contribute to acidification and local air pollution
SO_2, Sulphur dioxide, contribute to acidification and local air pollution
PM_{10}, Particulates, are airborne particulate matter that can be carried into the lungs

UK's International Priorities for Sustainable Development

UK's International Priorities for Sustainable Development	Lead Department(s) (other Departments involved)	High level target/Aim	Information source on delivery
Eliminate poverty in poor countries, in particular through achievement of the Millennium Development Goals (Millennium Assembly of the UN, 2000) ▶ *MDG1: Eradicate extreme poverty and hunger* ▶ *MDG2: Achieve universal primary education* ▶ *MDG3: Promote gender equality and empower women* ▶ *MDG4: Reduce child mortality* ▶ *MDG5: Improve maternal health* ▶ *MDG6: Combat HIV/AIDS, malaria and other diseases* ▶ *MDG7: ensure environmental sustainability* ▶ *MDG8: develop a global partnership for development*	DFID	DFID 2005-2008 PSA focussed on meeting Millennium Development Goals	www.dfid.gov.uk
Trade (WSSD & Doha) ▶ *Extend an open and rules based multilateral trading system.* ▶ *Improve market access for developing countries.* ▶ *Promote mutual supportiveness of trade liberalisation, environmental protection and sustainable development.* ▶ *Minimise any negative impacts of trade liberalisation for developing countries.* ▶ *Reduce level of trade distorting subsidies, particularly in agriculture and fisheries.*	DTI (Defra, FCO, DFID)	DTI, DFID shared PSA target: "Ensure that the EU secures significant reductions in EU and world trade barriers by 2008, leading to opportunities for developing countries and a more competitive Europe"	White Paper on Trade and Investment (July 2004). www.dti.gov.uk/ewt/whitepaper.htm

UK's International Priorities for Sustainable Development	Lead Department(s) (other Departments involved)	High level target/Aim	Information source on delivery
Finance (WSSD & Monterrey) ▸ *Recommitment to the Monterrey Consensus of the International Conference on Financing for Development (Monterrey, Mexico March 2002)*	DFID, HMT (FCO, Defra, ODPM)	DFID PSA 2005-2008 Objective IV Target 3 Improved effectiveness of the multilateral system.	www.dfid.gov.uk including White Paper: Making Globalisation Work for the Poor 2002.
Water and Sanitation (WSSD & MDGs) ▸ *Recommitment to achieve the MDG of halving, by 2015 the proportion of people without access to safe drinking water* ▸ *To halve, by 2015 the proportion of people without access to basic sanitation* ▸ *Develop integrated water resource management plans*	DFID (Defra, DTI, FCO)	DFID 2005-2008 PSA targets focused on meeting Millennium Development Goals, including MDG7 on environmental sustainability.	Water Action Plan www.dfid.gov.uk International Trade Strategy for the Water Sector defraweb/environment/water/internat/sustainable-water/pdf/trade-strategy.pdf
Continued integration of environmental issues into country-led poverty reduction processes (WSSD) ▸ *MDG7 target to integrate principles of sustainable development into countries policies and programmes*	DFID (Defra, FCO, HMT)	DFID 2005-2008 PSA targets focussed on meeting Millennium Development Goals, including MDG7 on environmental sustainability.	www.dfid.gov.uk

UK's International Priorities for Sustainable Development	Lead Department(s) (other Departments involved)	High level target/Aim	Information source on delivery
Sustainable consumption and production (SCP) patterns (WSSD) ➤ **More sustainable patterns of consumption and production** ➤ **Develop a 10 year framework of SCP programmes** ➤ **Reverse trend in loss of natural resources**	Defra, DTI (HMT, FCO, PM Strategy Unit, OGC(Procurement), ODPM)	Defra PSA 1 and key strategic outcomes[9]: "progress towards delivering the WSSD commitments notably in the areas of sustainable consumption and production chemicals, biodiversity, oceans, fisheries and agriculture"	Changing patterns – UK Government Framework for SCP http://www.defra.gov.uk/environment/business/scp/index.htm WSSD Delivery Plan http://www.sustainable-development.gov.uk/wssd2/08.htm
Renewable Energy; Energy efficiency (WSSD) ➤ **Urgently and substantially increase global use of renewable energy; increase energy efficiency**	DTI, Defra, FCO (PM Strategy Unit, ODPM, DFID)	Defra PSA 1 and key strategic outcomes[9]: "to promote sustainable development across government and in the UK and internationally as measured by….. ➤ progress towards delivering the WSSD commitments notably in the areas of sustainable consumption and production, chemicals, biodiversity, oceans, fisheries and agriculture ➤ progress towards internationally agreed commitments to tackle climate change"	Energy White Paper www.dti.gov.uk/energy/whitepaper/ourenergyfuture.pdf UK International Priorities: The Energy Strategy www.fco.gov.uk/Files/kfile/Energy_Report_281004.pdf Energy Efficiency Action Plan www.official-documents.co.uk/document/cm61/6168/6168.pdf Sustainable Energy Policy Network www.dti.gov.uk/energy/sepn/index.shtml Renewable Energy & Energy Efficiency Partnership www.reeep.org

[9] Defra 5 year strategy http://www.defra.gov.uk/corporate/5year-strategy/index.htm

UK's International Priorities for Sustainable Development	Lead Department(s) (other Departments involved)	High level target/Aim	Information source on delivery
Biodiversity and forestry (WSSD) ➤ **Significantly reduce rate of biodiversity loss by 2010** ➤ **Sharing benefits from and access to genetic resources** ➤ **Strengthen forest law enforcement and governance**	Defra, Forestry Commission (DFID, FCO, ODPM)	Defra PSA 1 and key strategic outcome "progress towards delivering the WSSD commitments notably in the areas of sustainable consumption and production, chemicals, biodiversity, oceans, fisheries and agriculture"	WSSD Delivery Plan www.sustainable-development.gov.uk/ wssd2/08.htm
Fisheries (WSSD) ➤ **Restore depleted fish stocks by 2015**	Defra (FCO, DFID, DTI, DfT (IMO))	Defra PSA 1 and key strategic outcome "progress towards delivering the WSSD commitments notably in the areas of sustainable consumption and production, chemicals, biodiversity, oceans, fisheries and agriculture"	WSSD Delivery Plan www.sustainable-development.gov.uk/ wssd2/08.htm
Chemicals (WSSD) ➤ **Minimise adverse effects of chemicals on human health and environment by 2020**	Defra (DH, DTI, HPA, HSE)	Defra PSA 1 and key strategic outcome "progress towards delivering the WSSD commitments notably in the areas of sustainable consumption and production, chemicals, biodiversity, oceans, fisheries and agriculture"	WSSD Delivery Plan www.sustainable-development.gov.uk/ wssd2/08.htm
Marine issues (WSSD) ➤ **Networks of marine protected areas by 2012**	Defra (FCO, DFID, DfT, DTI)	Defra PSA 1 and key strategic outcome "progress towards delivering the WSSD commitments notably in the areas of sustainable consumption and production, chemicals, biodiversity, oceans, fisheries and agriculture"	WSSD Delivery Plan www.sustainable-development.gov.uk/ wssd2/08.htm
Corporate Social Responsibility (WSSD) ➤ **Actively promote corporate social responsibility**	DTI[10]	The UK government will foster an enabling environment: for responsible business practice to maximise the positive contribution that business can make to the UK's objectives on international sustainable development – including human rights, trade and investment, poverty eradication, environmental protection and corruption – whilst at the same time effectively tackling adverse impact	International strategic Framework for Corporate Social Responsibility to be published in 2005 www.csr.gov.uk sets out the work of a number of different Government Departments

[10] Most other Government Departments are also involved in CSR.

UK's International Priorities for Sustainable Development	Lead Department(s) (other Departments involved)	High level target/Aim	Information source on delivery
Agriculture (WSSD & Doha) ➤ **Delivery of Doha Development Agenda commitments to reduce level of trade-distorting subsidies**	Defra (DTI)	Defra PSA 1 and key strategic outcome as above "progress towards delivering the WSSD commitments notably in the areas of sustainable consumption and production, chemicals, biodiversity, oceans, fisheries and agriculture"	WSSD Delivery Plan www.sustainable-development.gov.uk/wssd2/08.htm
International Sustainable Development Governance (WSSD) ➤ **Strengthen international environmental governance.** ➤ **Mainstream SD in UN and International Financial Institutions**	FCO, Defra (DFID)	FCO PSA 8 "To promote sustainable development, underpinned by democracy, good governance and human rights, particularly through effective delivery of programmes in these and related fields"	FCO Sustainable Development Strategy www.fco.gov.uk/sustainabledevelopment WSSD Delivery Plan www.fco.gov.uk/sustainabledevelopment
Fight against corruption and improve transparency ➤ **Strengthen the commitment of governments to implement international anti-corruption standards, including by ratifying UNCAC** ➤ **Improve transparency of extractives sector management in developing countries**	FCO/DFID	Strengthen implementation of international anti-corruption standards through strengthening anti-corruption capacity in developing countries	EITI (Extractive Industries Transparency Initiative) www.eitransparency.org FCO Sustainable Development Strategy www.fco.gov.uk/sustainabledevelopment
Environmental Governance and Human rights (WSSD) ➤ **Promote freedom of information, public participation in decision making and rule of law**	FCO (Defra, DFID)	FCO PSA 8 "To promote sustainable development, underpinned by democracy, good governance and human rights, particularly through effective delivery of programmes in these and related fields"	FCO Sustainable Development Strategy www.fco.gov.uk/sustainabledevelopment WSSD Delivery Plan www.fco.gov.uk/sustainabledevelopment

UK's International Priorities for Sustainable Development	Lead Department(s) (other Departments involved)	High level target/Aim	Information source on delivery
Access to energy (WSSD) ▶ **Provide reliable and affordable energy services.**	DFID (Defra, DTI, FCO)	DFID 2005-2008 PSA focussed on meeting Millennium Development Goals	'Energy for the Poor' www.dfid.gov.uk Renewable Energy & Energy Efficiency Partnership www.reeep.org
Partnerships (WSSD) ▶ **Enhance partnerships between governmental and non-governmental actors for the achievement of sustainable development.**	Defra (DFID, FCO, DTI, HMT, ODPM)	– *International* – ensure follow-up in UN system, particularly UN CSD, and further facilitation of partnerships – *UK* – continued monitoring and implementation of UK's partnership commitments; expansion as appropriate of existing initiatives	WSSD partnerships: www.sustainable-development.gov.uk/wssd2
Climate Change ▶ **Urge countries to ratify the Kyoto protocol.**	Defra (DTI, DfT, FCO, DFID)	Defra PSA 1 and key strategic outcome: "progress towards internationally agreed commitments to tackle climate change" The Energy White Paper: "work with other countries to establish both a consensus around the need for change and firm commitmer ts to take action to reduce carbon emissions world-wide within the framework of the UNFCCC" Key delivery mechanism will be international negotiations through the UNFCCC framework and the EU.	The Defra 5 year strategy www.defra.gov.uk/corporate/5year-strategy/index.htm Energy white paper: http://www.dti.gov.uk/energy/whitepaper/our energyfuture.pdf. UK International Priorities: The Energy Strategy www.co.gov.uk/files/kfile/Energy_Report_2 81004.pdf

UK's International Priorities for Sustainable Development	Lead Department(s) (other Departments involved)	High level target/Aim	Information source on delivery
Education (voluntary national commitment) *Progress towards all of the goals and priorities set out in the DfES international strategy:* ▶ *Goal 1: 'Equipping our children, young people and adults for life in a global society and work in a global economy'* ▶ *Goal 2: 'Engaging with our international partners to achieve their goals and ours'* ▶ *Goal 3: 'Maximising the contribution of our education and training sector, and university research to overseas trade and inward investment'*	DfES	Enabling every English school to establish a sustainable international school partnershp by 2010 Work with UN agencies, the World Bank and our G8, Commonwealth and EU partners to develop and offer educational support programmes, including policy and practitioner experts and information exchange, especially in Africa To raise the level of international awareness in schools through various means including an annual promotional exercise targeted at the education sector called International Education Week; and a new website called the Global Gateway which provides a school partner finding facility and comprehensive information on international dimensions to education	'Putting the World into World-Class Education – An international strategy for education, skills and children's services' www.globalgateway.org 'Sustainable development action plan for Education and Skills' www.teachernet.gov.uk/wholeschool/sd/actionplan An implementation plan for the strategy will be published in Spring 2005.

Annex A
Definition and Components of Sustainable Communities

Components: in full

Sustainable communities embody the principles of sustainable development.

They:
> *balance and integrate the social, economic and environmental components of their community*
> *meet the needs of existing and future generations*
> *respect the needs of other communities in the wider region or internationally also to make their communities sustainable.*

Sustainable communities are diverse, reflecting their local circumstances. There is no standard template to fit them all. But they should be:

(1) ACTIVE, INCLUSIVE AND SAFE – *fair, tolerant and cohesive with a strong local culture and other shared community activities*

Sustainable communities offer:
> a sense of community identity and belonging
> tolerance, respect and engagement with people from different cultures, background and beliefs
> friendly, co-operative and helpful behaviour in neighbourhoods
> opportunities for cultural, leisure, community, sport and other activities, including for children and young people
> low levels of crime, drugs and anti-social behaviour with visible, effective and community-friendly policing
> social inclusion and good life chances for all

(2) WELL RUN – *with effective and inclusive participation, representation and leadership*

Sustainable communities enjoy:
> representative, accountable governance systems which both facilitate strategic, visionary leadership and enable inclusive, active and effective participation by individuals and organisations
> effective engagement with the community at neighbourhood level, including capacity building to develop the community's skills, knowledge and confidence
> strong, informed and effective partnerships that lead by example (e.g. government, business, community)

> a strong, inclusive, community and voluntary sector
> a sense of civic values, responsibility and pride

(3) ENVIRONMENTALLY SENSITIVE – *providing places for people to live that are considerate of the environment*

Sustainable communities:
> actively seek to minimise climate change, including through energy efficiency and the use of renewables
> protect the environment, by minimising pollution on land, in water and in the air
> minimise waste and dispose of it in accordance with current good practice
> make efficient use of natural resources, encouraging sustainable production and consumption
> protect and improve bio-diversity (e.g. wildlife habitats)
> enable a lifestyle that minimises negative environmental impact and enhances positive impacts (e.g. by creating opportunities for walking and cycling, and reducing noise pollution and dependence on cars)
> create cleaner, safer and greener neighbourhoods (e.g. by reducing litter and graffiti, and maintaining pleasant public spaces)

(4) WELL DESIGNED AND BUILT – *featuring a quality built and natural environment*

Sustainable communities offer:
> a sense of place (e.g. a place with a positive 'feeling' for people and local distinctiveness)
> user-friendly public and green spaces with facilities for everyone including children and older people
> sufficient range, diversity, affordability and accessibility of housing within a balanced housing market
> appropriate size, scale, density, design and layout, including mixed-use development, that complement the distinctive local character of the community
> high quality, mixed-use, durable, flexible and adaptable buildings, using sustainable construction materials
> buildings and public spaces which promote health and are designed to reduce crime and make people feel safe
> accessibility of jobs, key services and facilities by public transport, walking and cycling

(5) WELL CONNECTED – *with good transport services and communication linking people to jobs, schools, health and other services*

Sustainable communities offer:
▶ transport facilities, including public transport, that help people travel within and between communities and reduce dependence on cars
▶ facilities to encourage safe local walking and cycling
▶ an appropriate level of local parking facilities in line with local plans to manage road traffic demand
▶ widely available and effective telecommunications and Internet access
▶ good access to regional, national and international communications networks

(6) THRIVING – *with a flourishing and diverse local economy*

Sustainable communities feature:
▶ a wide range of jobs and training opportunities
▶ sufficient suitable land and buildings to support economic prosperity and change
▶ dynamic job and business creation, with benefits for the local community
▶ a strong business community with links into the wider economy
▶ economically viable and attractive town centres

(7) WELL SERVED – *with public, private, community and voluntary services that are appropriate to people's needs and accessible to all*

Sustainable communities have:
▶ well-performing local schools, further and higher education institutions, and other opportunities for life-long learning
▶ high quality local health care and social services, integrated where possible with other services
▶ high quality services for families and children (including early years child care)
▶ a good range of affordable public, community, voluntary and private services (e.g. retail, fresh food, commercial, utilities, information and advice) which are accessible to the whole community
▶ service providers who think and act long term and beyond their own immediate geographical and interest boundaries, and who involve users and local residents in shaping their policy and practice

(8) FAIR FOR EVERYONE – *including those in other communities, now and in the future*

Sustainable communities:
▶ recognise individuals' rights and responsibilities
▶ respect the rights and aspirations of others (both neighbouring communities, and across the wider world) also to be sustainable
▶ have due regard for the needs of future generations in current decisions and actions

Printed in the UK for The Stationery Office Limited
on behalf of the Controller of Her Majesty's Stationery Office
03/05,176844
Printed on recycled paper containing 80% post consumer waste & 20% totally chlorine free virgin pulp